7 Ways to Grow Rich!

7 Essential Traits Every Winner Must Have

Mahubo Fabulous

ISBN 978-0-578-16486-1

DEDICATION

I dedicate this book to the motivational coaches who have inspired me to serve people and help them find their life's purpose and passion.

Contents

ACKNOWLEDGMENTS

The unwavering support of the following people made publishing "7 Ways to Grow Rich" a transforming journey. I would like to thank Abdi Mahad who willingly shared different perspectives when the idea of the book was conceived. Isnino Aga for pushing me to stay focused and saw a potential when I didn't. Ascanio Pignatelli Leadership Coach (www.leadfromneed.com) who was interviewed for the leadership chapter, thank you for the valuable information provided and your contribution to the book. Thank you my amazing cat Meeko who made breaks between writing sessions something to look forward to. My editor Yasmin Ali who shaped my ideas and brought them to life under a clear and concise manner. Thank you Jefferson Jivoli for the design of the cover, your professional feedback eased my mind.

Introduction

7 Ways to Grow Rich!

Your 7-step guide to build more richness than money can buy.

If the secret to riches was taking up a second job, working multiple shifts, or slogging away at the desk, then most of us would be rolling in money right now. Fortunately, you don't have to waste away to grow money like a tree.

7 Ways to Grow Rich! unfolds the master plan. It is your 7-step success guide to help you break away from attitudes and behaviors that keep away abundance. Learn how to set the Law of Attraction in motion and draw wealth and abundance into your life. Get the low-down on how to earn money even as you sleep. Become the best version of yourself.

7 Ways to Grow Rich! seeks to transform you from the inside out, so you become a magnet for wealth, abundance, and prosperity. Apparently, not all lessons are taught in B-schools!

Isn't it a wonder how money always seems to be in short supply?

And no, it's not only you who has a hard time holding on to the money that comes in. Ask anybody around you, and you will get the same exasperated query, "Will my financial woes never end?"

So how much money is enough?

But can you really put a number to your monetary needs? After all, your life situation changes through the years. Your goals change accordingly. So do your aspirations.

The amount of money that seemed princely when you were in college turns out to be pitifully low when you have a growing family to feed.

Then there is inflation. It always changes equations and leaves us with less than what we need to survive.

So instead of trying to figure out how much you should earn, let's take the easy way out. BE RICH!

Become so rich that all your money troubles vanish.

Become rich enough to quit the job you hate and the boss you despise and embrace a life where you can live on your own terms.

Become so rich that you never ever have to worry about how to pay the bills or when you will land the next gig.

Become rich enough to retire early and travel the world.

Make so much money that you don't have to worry about money anymore.

Attaining financial freedom is not pie in the sky. Many people have. And they were not born with silver spoons in their mouths. They didn't land an inheritance. Nor are they blessed with superhuman talents and abilities. They are average people like you, with average problems and going through more or less similar life situations.

But … they had dreams.

They dreamed of becoming rich. They wanted to take back control of their lives. They so badly wanted their dreams to come true that they took matters into their own hands.

You can too!

There is no money to be coughed up. You don't have to go through school again. You can work at your day job *(Only for now.)* and pursue money-making activities *(Yes, the riches show up almost instantly.)* on the side. Or you can quit your job and plunge headlong into the riches pool that is waiting for you.

Just read this book. *7 Ways to Grow Rich!*

Yes, there are only seven steps before a world of abundance and prosperity opens up in front of you. It's not a get-rich-quick scheme; those don't work. It's also not any long drawn-out affair that will take years to show results. It's just a collection of seven simple steps that will transform you into a magnet for money and attract riches into your life.

7 Ways to Grow Rich! works on you, your beliefs and attitudes, and your way of working. It aligns your disparate selves, so you can combine all your energies to attract riches into your life.

The book delineates steps to transform you into a powerful mass of throbbing, vibrant energy that attracts collaborators, business partners, and other influential people who can guide you along the path to your dreams. These are DIY self-improvement measures that you will want to learn and imbibe to become the best version of yourself.

The book describes fundamental leadership skills that will help you rise to the top and take charge of people and situations.

The book explores ways of making money without wasting away working late hours or multiple shifts. You will learn about easy-to-set-up passive income streams that will keep bringing in money even when you sleep!

7 Ways to Grow Rich! is your one-stop how-to guide to a life of riches. And while you are at it, the book also helps you become more resourceful, courageous, insightful, wise, and compassionate. You see, the *riches* indicated in the title are not just monetary riches.

The book takes you on a journey of self-discovery, self-mastery, and self-improvement that is essential to attain spiritual bliss and mental peace. Now, are these not *riches* too?

7 Ways to Grow Rich! is the only book out there that takes a comprehensive holistic and sustainable approach to money-making.

Do you think it is pure chance that you came by this book? No, you are the Chosen One because it is NOW time that you claimed the abundance you deserve.

Happy   reading!

1.

How to Set Goals and Nail Them

Crystallize your goals. Make a plan for achieving them and set yourself a deadline. Then, with supreme confidence, determination and disregard for obstacles and other people's criticisms, carry out your plan.---Paul J. Meyer

Look at all the successful people around you—the ones who have made it big.

The mom-and-pop store owners who now rule over a national chain of outlets. The ex-corporate professional who quit his soul-sucking job to launch his dream business and live a six-figure lifestyle. The girl who battled poverty and homelessness during her childhood and now has hundreds of people working for her. The stories of these heroes and heroines have taken different paths. But dig deeper, and you will find a pattern.

These people did not get to where there are now by moping and whining about their misfortunes. Nor were they wallowing in self-pity. They didn't let depression and frustration get the better of them. Instead, they busied themselves setting goals and chasing them down.

Goals. Setting goals and chasing them smartly. This is what separates the super-achievers from the also-rans. Not everyone is born with a silver spoon in mouth. Nor do opportunities fall on the lap of all. But some people create a life of their dreams despite their adversities. That's because these people focus their energies on rising above challenges and getting to their goals.

Thankfully, setting and achieving goals is not a special talent that rich people are born with. There is a definite formula for goal-setting success, and it is not rocket science. All successful people, whatever be their IQs and educational attainments, follow this goal-setting formula to shine in life. You can too.

Here's the step list, assuming that you know where you want to go in life:

1. Set specific goals.

You have only so much time, energy, and resources. Make sure that you don't waste them doing sundry unimportant tasks that go about looking like "urgent" jobs but actually don't help you get any closer to your dream. You have to set specific goals, so you can focus your efforts.

You want to be rich. But this is not a specific goal; it is a fond dream that will keep you motivated as you strive to carve out a life of abundance and prosperity. Set more specific goals that tell you what you need to do to become rich. Here are some pointers:

- You are in a 9-to-5 job and have no plans to quit anytime soon. After all, knowing that you have a steady paycheck to fall back on does feel reassuring. So if you want to make pots of money, you might want to take up a second job. Maybe you can moonlight as a blogger or launch your own business that brings in supplemental income. So set specific goals like, "I will set up my bakery business" or "I will work part-time as a writer or a consultant."

- If you own a business, set specific goals like adding a new line of products, setting up more stores in your state, or using social media to attract customers. "I will grow my business" is a vague goal that doesn't provide any direction.

- If you want to become rich by investing smartly, set specific goals like "I will trade in stocks and bonds" instead of something vague like "I will diversify my investment portfolio" that does not tell you anything about what you should do.

2. Set measurable goals.

Add numbers to your goals. Deadlines, sales figures, and profit margins give you a sense of urgency and help you pace your efforts and set up routines. Later on, these numbers will help you evaluate your performance.

So add deadlines to your goals, like "I will set up two more stores within the next six months" or "I will sell 1,000 pieces of my handmade bags in three months." With these numbers looming large in front of you, your sub-conscious mind will automatically push you to reach for them. You will be less likely to procrastinate or slack off.

3. Set performance goals instead of outcome goals.

Many amongst us are results-driven individuals. We tend to measure our success and failure *(and feel good or bad about ourselves)* based on the results that show up. But we do not live in an idyllic world. Here results do not always reflect the efforts we put into a job. You may have all the degrees and stellar references, but the plum job can still go to the most experienced candidate. A storm, a flood, or a riot can prevent you from delivering the orders on time. Sometimes, things, people, and situations are out of our control. So don't be obsessed with outcomes.

In some cases, setting performance goals instead of outcome goals will help you keep away disappointment and remain motivated. So how do performance goals keep you on course on the road to riches? Here's one instance.

You can set an outcome goal like "I will break even and start making profits within five years of setting up my business." But what if the economy goes on a downswing just after you launch your business? What if your customers feel the pocket pinch of raised taxes or increased gasoline prices and are compelled to cut back their spending? In such circumstances, you cannot let yourself lose heart and back out just because you did not meet your outcome goal.

At these times, you can set sustainable performance goals like "I will provide quality products" or " I will streamline the production process, so I can provide my goods at lower prices." Such goals ensure that you remain on top of your game whatever be the circumstances around you. Your dedication to quality will eventually bring you more customers in the long run.

4. Identify smaller sub-goals using the Backward Planning Method.

Realizing your goals is not doing just one thing right. Your grand plan is made up of a series of small tasks. You cannot launch your dream business with only a press of a button. You have to set up a storefront, market your products, reach out to your customers, manufacture the goods, and send out free samples before the orders start pouring in. These are the sub-goals that will eventually turn you into the business baron you had always dreamed of becoming.

Try the Backward Planning method to identify the sub-goals. Say, you want financial independence. You want to be able to quit your job but still have the money coming in as you pursue your passion. This is your Big Goal.

Now what do you need to do to reach this goal? *You have to create a passive income stream.*

What can you do to create a passive income stream? *Find out how you can make money from your passion.*

How can you find the time to engage in your passion? *Quit your job or work part-time.*

How will you pay the bills and put food on the table when you are not earning as much as before or none at all? *Start saving from today to build a rainy-day fund.*

How can you lessen your financial burden so that the rainy-day funds last long? *Reorganize the domestic budget, so you can save more and pay off the debts quickly.*

There you are, you now have a list of sub-goals.. When you try the Backward Planning method, you arrive at all the tasks you have to carry out to reach your Big Goal.

5. Set realistic goals.

Set your goals, but be realistic. Reaching a milestone feels motivating, but it is equally discouraging when you fail to make the mark despite slogging away. Don't set yourself up for failure and frustration by setting the bar too high. Here's what to remember when you set your goals:

- Set your goals in keeping with your available resources. For instance, take on orders depending on the capacity of your production unit.

- Set your goals keeping in mind your personal responsibilities and obligations. For instance, if you have little kids or a family member who is ill, plan your business duties so that you can also spend time at home. Remember, all the riches in the world cannot equal the company of your loved ones.

- Set your goals depending on your physical and mental capabilities. Burn the midnight oil and keep your nose to the grindstone, but don't burn out. Know how much to take on and when to stop. If you have to learn new skills, allow yourself time to master the learning curve and set deadlines accordingly.

- Set your goals to account for some me-time. The race to the riches is tough, but you also need to take care of your body, mind, and soul. Weave some downtime into your plans when you can pamper yourself and return to the race rejuvenated.

6. Prioritize your goals.

When you identify the set of sub-goals that will take you to your dreams, the list might look overwhelming. Yes, it takes a lot to reach your dreams, but you don't have to get started on everything at the same time. Ask any achiever; taking on more than what you can manage and stretching yourself too thin won't get you to success. Instead, you risk messing up on all fronts. So focus. Prioritize your goals.

Here's what to keep in mind when you prioritize goals:

- Accord the highest priority to the critical goals that will help you reach other goals. For instance, you want to launch your own money-making blog and earn six figures from it. For this, you will have to make the time to create quality posts regularly and take to the social media to spread the word about your blog.

- Take on the easy goals first and get them out of the way. Every tick on the to-do list will boost your confidence.

- Prioritize sub-goals for which you have the resources available. Because you won't have to scout for resources, you will reach these goals quicker and get closer to your Big Goal.

7. Identify the resources you need en route to your goals.

You have drive, determination, oodles of motivation, and boundless energy. But you also need other resources to get to your goals. Here's a list:

- **Time:** If you are reading this book now, it is likely that what you are doing for living is not bringing you the riches you desire. You will either have to do more of what you are doing now, change jobs, or work on the side. You need time. Plan how you can squeeze time from your daily schedule to accommodate a few hours to work on more assignments or take up a second job.

- **Materials:** If you plan to launch your own business, you have to secure the necessary permits and licenses, set up a production unit, recruit people, and buy the raw materials and equipment to start manufacturing. Whatever be your strategy to grow rich, you will need land, labor, equipment, or raw materials to deliver your offerings.

- **Skills:** Riches come to those who are perceived to be the best in their respective niches. You have to hone your skills or add to your existing skill set to stand out from competition and impress your clients.

- **Money:** Money makes the world go round. So whatever be your get-rich strategy, you will have to invest some money right at the outset to get the ball rolling. You need money to buy materials, enroll in a course to learn a new skill, buy inventory and retail space, pay your workers and suppliers, and market your offerings.

- **Health:** Health is wealth. Whoever coined this phrase obviously knew how critical it is for you to maintain good health as you strive to reach your goals. You have to work long and hard to build your riches, and you need all the energy you can muster to go full throttle.

- **Support Systems:** No man is an island. We all have to depend on one another to survive and prosper. So don't hesitate to ask for help from friends and family. You need a support network to fall back on when you cannot cope single-handedly. You may need someone to babysit when you are away on a business lunch, run your errands as you try to finish your assignments, or give you a pep talk when you feel the blues.

You may have to create mini-plans to gather resources like money, time, and health. But these are the sauces to your success, so get going.

8. Look at your habits closely. Modify, if you need to.

Do you remember the book *The 7 Habits of Highly Effective People* that came out a few decades ago? You probably do because this work is regarded as a seminal work in business and self-help literature. It sold tens of millions of copies when it was first published. It still flies off the shelves, and people lap it up eagerly.

Do you notice the word "habits" in the title?

The author, Stephen Covey, wants us to emulate the habits of successful people because he believes habits can make or break your chances of reaching your goals. And no, he was not referring to bad habits like drinking or gambling. In his book, he talks about the good habits that make you more effective and warns you about the negative ones that bring on chaos. Good habits are powerful productivity tools because they can turn you into a lean, mean machine that delivers results consistently. Bad habits do the opposite. Unfortunately, not many people realize this, and forming good habits and banishing the negative ones do not form a part of their goal-setting and goal-getting agendas.

For instance, exercising regularly, eating nutritious food, meditating, and being in the moment help you stay healthy, be calm, and focus on the work at hand. You should turn these good practices into habits to become more productive. These habits not only help you attract riches but also enhance the quality of your life in other ways as well.

Here's how you can identify the good habits that will help you reach your goals and the bad habits, if any, that you need to banish from your life:

- Find out how you can be more productive. If you are a morning person, then cultivate the habit of waking up early, so you can get the most work done when you are at your peak.

- Figure out what keeps you from being productive. Is it spending too much time on Facebook? You can try to break your habit by disconnecting the Internet when you are at work.

- Find out the root cause behind your unproductive habits. It may be that you regularly take on too much work that makes you falter in the end. You have to learn to say "No" more often.

There is a saying that we are creatures of habits. It is both good and bad. The bad is that it takes some time to undo old habits; you have to keep at it diligently. But the good thing is that once you have formed the good habits, they will stay with you for long. Start small, cultivate one good habit at a time, and be patient.

9. Create a step-by-step plan.

Now that you have identified all that you need to gather and do to reach your goals, create a game plan. This would be a map of sorts that will guide you along the right track and keep you focused and on course to success. Here's what to include in your strategy:

- A list of your goals and sub-goals in the order of their priorities and along with their deadlines

- A list of the resources you need to achieve your goals

- A list of what you need to do to gather these resources

- The bad habits you need to banish from your life

- The strategy to break bad habits

- The good habits you need to cultivate

- The strategy to cultivate and sustain the good habits

- A list of the roadblocks you may face along the way

- An action plan to tackle every roadblock

Now create Plan B because you do not know when the taxation laws will change, which way the economy will swing, what the financial planners have in mind, or how the political situation in another country shapes up to affect the demand for your offerings or the supply of raw materials. It is always good to have a backup plan.

10. Re-assess your goals and plans periodically.

Use your Moleskin, a fancy productivity app, or the good old Excel spreadsheet to track your progress regularly and ensure you are on course. Don't forget to give yourself a pat on the back or a treat every time you reach a milestone.

Tracking also helps you re-evaluate your goals and plans in the light of what's happening in your life and around you.

We live in an ever-changing world. The volatility is especially palpable in matters of wealth. Whether it is the real estate market or the stock market, expect sudden swings, spikes, and meltdowns regularly. Your fortunes are intricately tied to the whims of the market, local, national, or global. So you have to not only keep abreast of what is happening in these markets but also tweak your goals and strategies accordingly. Also be prepared to modify your goals and plans based on the needs of your growing family or your changed priorities in life.

You can attract riches in your life in two ways. You can wait for good opportunities to sprout and the winds to shift in your favor to make a grab. Or you can take charge of your fate, create your own opportunities, and march towards them boldly. If you are the go-getter type, start setting goals now.

2.

How to Find Your Passion and Live It

"Passion is energy. Feel the power that comes from focusing on what excites you."--Oprah Winfrey

Those get-rich-quick schemes don't work. You have to work hard to build your wealth.

The business barons with their flourishing empires work long and hard to keep up with the industry trends and innovate. The Hollywood stars, who earn millions of dollars doing one movie, shoot for hours on end just to film one scene, train hard at the gym to keep fit and flab-free, and continuously hone their skills to keep bagging plum offers. The blogger with a money-minting blog has to keep himself updated on the developments in his niche, conjure up and write new posts every other day, dish out freebies for his readers, and relentlessly market his site on the social media.

Those who seem to have it all still have to work hard. It is a dog-eat-dog world out there; nobody can afford to rest on their laurels.

So what keeps these successful men and women going even when they are about to drop dead with exhaustion and fatigue? How do they keep themselves motivated when the chips are down? What inspires them to get up, pick up the pieces, and keep moving every time they fall?

PASSION.

You can set as many goals as you like and follow them doggedly. But it is passion that will keep you going on the days when you lack motivation or the results seem elusive.

Passion will motivate you to carry on when those who were supposed to have your back throw a spanner in the works.

Passion will keep you energized and enthusiastic when the to-do list seems overwhelming and all you want to do is give up, bow out, and go back to the job you hated so much.

What Keeps Us Away from Our Passions?

We work long hours, but we resent every moment of it. We take up one project after another, but the work does not inspire us. We crib about our bosses, the deadlines, and our co-workers. Yet we keep going back to the 9-to-5 jobs we hate because we feel compelled to go by society's expectations.

If you have a family, you have to stick to your "steady" job; forget about investing your money in your dream business.

If you want to live comfortably in your sunset years, deny yourself all pleasures now and save every penny for the future.

A good life is one where you bag a plum, cushy corporate job that comes with health insurance and sundry other perks.

Our society has laid down pretty strict rules about how we should go about our lives. It has its own notion of what success should look like. In our heart of hearts, we feel these definitions are narrow and the rules, too stringent. But we play on.

Why?

Fear of Society's Backlash

As social animals, we yearn for acceptance by our fellow human beings. We want to belong to groups and close to other people. And we have come to believe that conformity breeds acceptance because we know how society treats individuals who choose authenticity over convention.

People who choose to go against society's accepted norms and conventions and be themselves get tagged as "rebels," a label that is full of negative connotations. They are treated as outcasts. They have very few friends, and even fewer people empathize with them.

So, most of us choose not to stick out from the crowd. We decide not to be our authentic selves and follow our passions.

But...

Do you realize you are unhappy because you are not being your authentic self? We have been sent to this world to fulfill our unique life purposes. Our callings are different. So it is no wonder we are unhappy when we do not answer our soul's deepest desires.

Do you realize that by holding on to society's beliefs, you are actually holding yourself back? There is nothing wrong with society's beliefs. But they may not be the right choices for you. After all, we are unique individuals, and we are here to fulfill our specific destinies. By sticking to somebody else's vision of "perfect," we do not fulfill our true potential.

The Monday morning blues. The constant yearning to be someplace else rather than here. A longing for the times gone by. The relentless mental stress and fatigue. An aching feeling that something is missing from your life. These are the tell-tale signs that you are not happy with how your life is unfolding right now.

Fear of Failure

We all know how our society treats people who it considers as "failures" by its yardstick. The looks of pity and the brush-offs sting, and it is natural that we wouldn't wish this fate upon ourselves. So we play safe.

We stick to tried-and-tested methods instead of taking the off-beat route to explore uncharted territories. We stymie our dreams to live somebody else's dream because we are afraid of getting labeled as failures.

So the business idea that could have churned out millions of dollars in revenues remains a fond dream. The plot for a novel that could have been a bestseller never reaches the publisher.

But look around you.

Did the fear of failing prevent the young entrepreneur from launching his own business? His friends, family, and co-workers could not persuade him to stay in his six-figure job. He remained undaunted through all the hiccups and roadblocks of running a startup and making it yield profits.

Did the fear of failing prevent the Ivy League graduate from turning his back on a cushy corporate job and make a career in music? His albums now top the charts regularly, but he remembers his long and hard days of struggle. Clearly, he didn't let rejections and discouragement talk him out of his dream.

If these heroes had paid heed to their fears, they could not have carved a life of riches for themselves. They resolved to follow their passions boldly, come what may.

How to Live Passionately

Society's diktats, your fear of failure, the expectations from you by your near and dear ones, and the societal perception of success are sheer distractions. These cloud your judgment, dent your confidence in your abilities, and keep you from discovering your heart's desire. Your passion lies inside of you. You have to make the journey inward to discover it.

Here's how you can discover your passion and live it:

1. Know yourself.

Your passions are shaped by your unique likes and dislikes, experiences, values you hold dear, your perception of what "success" looks like, and the way you want to work and play for the rest of your life. You have to know yourself before you can unearth your passion.

Here are some tips:

- Figure out what motivates you and makes you tick. Does a fiercely-competitive, fast-paced, and deadline-driven world of business bring out the best in you? Then you will thrive in the edgy world of business where you have to be on your toes constantly. If you are a laidback person by nature, then you will likely find your passion in a job that lets you work from the quiet confines of your home or studio.

- Figure out what saps your mental energies and robs you of your peace of mind. If punishing work hours frustrate you and leave you hankering for some me-time, then consider quitting your job. You will thrive doing something else. If you are tired of having fools for bosses or managers who stress you out, then look for ways to strike out on your own where you can be own boss and set your own deadlines.

2. Find out about your interests and hobbies.

A saying goes that enthusiasm marks the difference between success and failure. Your interests and hobbies can provide the biggest clues about your passion.

Here's how to delve deeper into your interests to find out if you are really passionate about them:

- Are there subjects that interest you so much that you read up everything on them? The blogs and magazines you read, the online communities you are a member of and actively take part in, the groups you belong to, and the types of television shows you watch could provide a clue about your interest areas. If you spot a pattern, you are a step closer to nailing down your passion.

- Your hobbies, especially the ones you have managed to sustain despite the daily challenges you face, hold a clue to what you are passionate about. Do you find the time and energy to work away in your garden after a back-breaking and nerve-wracking day in office? Then you can consider starting a nursery. Have you held on to a childhood hobby and still pursue it even if it means being awake till the wee hours or forgoing parties and outings? Then you should explore ways to turn your hobby into a money-making pursuit.

- Think about all the jobs that you do right now that energize you mentally. Think of all the jobs you do to make a living, for love, and out of duty.

- Do you look forward to any work? Does the mere thought of working at something excite you so much that you are ready to jump into it right away?

3. Find out what you are effortlessly good at.

Look at all the successful men and women around you. They may work in different industries, but they share a common trait. They look effortlessly good at what they do. Be assured that they put in lots of hard work into what they do, but the struggle doesn't show. It is as if they were born to do this work. And maybe they were.

We are usually effortlessly good at what we are passionate about. Our passions sharpen our focus and intuition, energize us so we can keep up with the trends, and make us enthusiastic about dreaming up new projects and seeing them through to completion. We usually end up doing a stellar job of what we are enthusiastic about.

If you cannot figure out the jobs you are effortlessly good at, your friends, family members, or co-workers can guide you. At times, they can be a better judge of your capabilities than you are.

4. Hark back to your childhood.

We outgrow many childhood habits and interests, but that spark of passion we felt for certain things stays on somewhere within us. If you were the adventurous type in your childhood and dreamed of running away to the sea to become a sailor or fly an airplane, it is likely that your soul still yearns to be outdoors and take on the elements. Go back to your childhood to discover your passion.

Here's how:

- Think of your school days. Were there subjects you excelled in? Were you the one who always got straight A's in Geography? You have a feel for places; why don't you think of starting a business in travel and tourism?

- Think of your interests as a kid. What was that one thing that you looked forward to throughout the week? Were you willing to give up even play to indulge in your hobbies?

- Are you still lovingly clinging on to a childhood dream? You have outgrown the Superman dream, but do you still hope that someday you will be able to travel the world or own your own photography business? Do you browse through travel magazines and sigh wistfully at the colorful spreads? Then maybe it is time you tested your business idea.

5. Think about your favorite celebrities and the work they do.

We all have our heroes. We marvel at their lifestyles, admire them for the work they do, and live vicariously through them.

Our heroes are not always Hollywood A-listers or celebrities who make it to the covers of *Forbes* and *Time*. They may be a former co-worker who now runs his own flourishing farm or a neighbor who gave up her job as a successful lawyer to follow her jewelry-making dream.

If you find yourself constantly longing wistfully to live their lives, then consider following suit. If you want to be in their shoes, then you probably should.

Remember, your heroes are not wired any differently than you are; the difference is in the passion they bring to their jobs and the courage they show to stick to their vocations despite setbacks.

6. Figure out if there's anything you will do for free.

You don't have to do it forever. In fact, not even for a day. Just imagine doing something for free.

Think of your favorite pastimes, hobbies, and interests. Take up one and imagine you are doing it for free for the rest of your life. Keep away all thoughts of bills and mortgages while you are daydreaming; else you will miss out on the fun!

Remember you are not getting paid for the work you do. Don't expect a promotion. Nor will pats on the back, awards, and medals come your way. The world at large may not even know you are creating masterpieces.

How does the dream feel like? Do you feel motivated to take up the work? Are you willing to slog away at it without expecting any return? If you have answered "Yes," you have nailed down your passion.

7. Find out if there is anything that you will regret not doing during your lifetime.

Imagine it is your last day in this world.

That's a scary thought. But we all need a jolt (read: reality check) to brush the cobwebs from our minds, look beyond illusions, ignore society's demands and expectations, and find true meaning and abiding value.

Take up one fond dream of yours and imagine not doing this ever in your life. How does it feel like? Do you feel overwhelming sadness or pangs of bitterness? Does it feel that you have wasted your life doing meaningless tasks? Do you feel you have not fulfilled your true potential? If such thoughts trouble you, it is time to stop doing what you are wasting away at and concentrate on your passion because you have just discovered it.

Do this exercise for all your dreams. Ask yourself questions, and trust that your heart will show you the way.

8. Explore ways you can make money from your passion.

Congratulations on discovering your passion in life! Not many people are as fortunate as you are. Some spend their lifetimes searching for meaning in life. Others hop from one job to another finding neither passion nor prosperity.

But now that you know what you want to do in life, it is time to step out from your mind—remember, you were on a journey into your heart and soul—and look at reality around you. You want to make money from your passion. And lots of it!

How can you turn your passion into a money-minting profession? Here are some tips:

- Pore over trade and industry journals and browse websites to find out about the different avenues that will let you make money from your passion.

- Ask around amongst your acquaintances or connect with people on the social media (Try LinkedIn.) to learn ways in which you make your passion pay your bills. Get in touch with business men or entrepreneurs who are living their dreams and doing something that you would love to do too. Passion shows and it is contagious. Who knows, these influential people might even take you under their wings to help you break free and soar high eventually.

- Speak to local businesses in your niche and recruiters to find out about job opportunities that will let you learn the tricks of the trade. After all, you need to get a hang of the industry before you can master its ways of working.

- Consider passive ways to build your income stream from your passion. You will be surprised to learn how easy it is to make money while you sleep! But more on this later.

- Consider taking up a second line of work that will let you indulge in your passion and also bring in some money. It is not always possible for everyone to quit their jobs and jump headlong into a new venture. A second job will let you test the waters without drying up the income stream.

9. Hone your skills.

You know why producers pay millions to certain actors and actresses for a single film. Because they know these stars will get under the skin of their characters, bring to life the plot, and make a movie worth watching many times over.

You know why publishers pay millions to authors even before they have penned a single chapter. Because they know these writers will not only draw in readers but also keep them captivated with their words.

Do you see a pattern here? Those who make money pursuing their passion do so by dint of their special skills. They stand out from competition with their unique offerings. It is no wonder they make riches because their clients are happy to shell out money for expertise.

You have to build your skills and diversify your offerings, so clients choose you over your competitors. You have to become an expert in what you do, so your clients keep returning to you. Here's how you can be on the top of your game:

- Talk to the experts in your field to learn how you can improve your skill set.

- Find out about the certifications you have to acquire that will establish you as an expert in your industry.

- Read trade journals, attend meetups, and network with the thought leaders and change agents in your industry to keep up with the trends and developments.

- Innovate. Innovate. Innovate.

- Keep offering more to your clients. Provide more expertise and suggest novel and cost-effective solutions to your clients.

10.   Set goals.

You know how to set goals and chase them down. Now that you have discovered your passion, start setting goals to get going. But before you fish out your smartphone or open a spreadsheet, here are a few pointers to help you keep away the stress of chasing goals:

- Remember, Rome was not built in a day. So, don't expect results to show up overnight. Give yourself time to master the learning curve and find your footing.

- It is okay not being able to devote the time you would have liked to to your dreams. Most of us are not footloose and fancy-free. We have families to take care of and professional obligations to meet. So carve out as much time you can manage to chase your goals. You can be slow and steady and still win the race.

- Don't compare yourself to others. We are all separate individuals with unique ways of working and peculiar life situations. So we are not supposed to cross the finishing line at the same time. Remind yourself that putting in small doses of effort consistently will get you to your goals sooner than sporadic bursts of activity.

When you discover your passion, it will not let you rest easy till you plunge into it. Passion is potent. It not only fuels you from the inside but also radiates outward to attract riches. Passionate people are self-motivated and they inspire others to seek collaborations.

3.

How to Prepare Your Mind to be Positive

He who limps is still walking.-- Stanislaw J. Lec

Do you know what lies between you and all the riches out there in the world that are up for grabs? Your mind. It can play the spoilsport in ways you may not realize.

What is the secret sauce in all rags-to-riches stories? Again, the mind. The human mind is an incredibly powerful tool that can recreate reality and make your dreams come true.

The mind is a double-edged sword.

You can make it bow to your wishes. It is so powerful that it can bend reality and attract abundance into your life whatever be your current station in life, bank balance, educational attainments, or the state of the economy.

But the mind can be mischievous too. If you let it have its way, it can trick you into sabotaging your chances of attracting riches into your life. And you wouldn't even realize that you have become your own worst enemy!

31

You have to learn to control the unruly mind before you can tap into its limitless reservoir of power.

The Sub-Conscious Mind and Positive Energy

The sub-conscious mind is a magnet for all the energies swirling around and flowing past you.

There is positive energy in happy and optimistic people, sunsets, a gurgling stream, funny cat videos, the sight of children playing with gay abandon, and inspirational stories of men and women who overcame odds to create a life of their dreams.

On the other hand, there is negative energy in the criticisms of people, discouraging words, fatalistic attitudes projected by others around you, and stories of despair and doom. And to add to the woes, we ourselves create negative energies by wallowing in feelings of depression, frustration, hate, jealousy, and self-pity.

We are constantly bombarded by the positive and negative vibes around us. The mind gobbles up these energies. Unfortunately, when we feed on too much negative energy, our own minds become stumbling blocks in the path to our progress. A negative mindset holds us back from attracting the riches we want in our lives.

The sunniest person in your office has the most friends. Your co-worker, scrambling up the corporate ladder, is a go-getter who never shies away from taking up new projects. Your favorite player goes into a game truly believing he will come out trumps, and he does. These are instances of people exuding positive energy to get what they want. These people don't focus on negative emotions like self-pity, fear, and hopelessness. And they have a reason.

A smile befriends strangers. Optimism and enthusiasm make other people want to collaborate with you. Positive energy makes the world go round; it attracts friends, clients, fame, and riches.

Positivity is powerful.

How to Cultivate Positive Mind

There is no one quality that is the hallmark of a positive mind. A positive mind is enthusiastic, optimistic, agile, responsive, self-confident, and self-possessed. You are lucky; positive energy is not determined by genes, upbringing, or educational achievements. Nor do you have to buy it. You can cultivate a positive mind with just a little practice.

Here's what you need to do:

1. Believe in the Law of Attraction.

There is a reason why people harp on the phrase "Mind over matter." The mind can certainly triumph over the body by morphing reality with its thoughts.

We all know of people who have overcame the physical and mental trauma of losing limbs to go on to hold steady jobs, raise happy families, and take part in competitive sports. Cancer patients overcome excruciating pain to lead joyful, productive, and inspiring lives. And then there are the people who survive abusive childhood, poverty, and deprivation to go on to become heads of multinational organizations or leaders of nations. These people do not let physical ailments, wants, circumstances, or the lack of encouragement or opportunities to come in their way.

How?

By setting into motion the Law of Attraction.

According to the Law of Attraction, we can attract abundance into our lives just by wishing for it. Wealth, fame, meaningful relationships, a house in the suburbs with white picket fence or a luxurious condo in an upscale part of the town, a gleaming toy in the garage, and a hefty bank balance—we can get anything we want. But, of course, you have to believe in the law to make it work for you.

The Law of Attraction is a powerful productivity tool. Believe in it and get on with whatever you are doing without worrying about the outcome or fearing failure. When you are stress-free, you can be more productive and embrace change readily. When you believe that the Law of Attraction will work for you, the enthusiasm shows in your work. Your conviction, hard work, and the natural workings of the Law will eventually bear fruit.

2. Believe in the goodness and wisdom of your Higher Self.

Yes, there's a Self that you didn't know about. But your Higher Self is not a separate entity; it is a part of you. It is that untapped part of your consciousness that is connected to the infinite reserves of wisdom, insights, and power of the Universe. So your Higher Self is a wise being that knows what is right for you. It loves you *(After all, it is the "real" you.)* and wants you to achieve your full potential and realize your dreams.

Your Higher Self goes by many names. Higher Consciousness, Universal Consciousness, the all-knowing Sub-Conscious Mind. Whatever you choose to call your Higher Self, trust that it has your back. And how do you know?

Hark back to all those times when a gut feeling saved you from signing a bad deal. Think about those times when the bad vibes you felt about a person turned out to be right. These were instances when your Higher Self got in touch with you to warn you and keep you out of harm's way. The Higher Self communicates through such subtle signals. It is up to you to believe in its presence, so it is encouraged to send out stronger signals.

Your Higher Self is your best friend. It sticks with you through thick and thin and guides you on your way to abundance. It is more powerful than your business associates. It loves you more than your BFF. It knows you better than you do. It knows what makes you tick, what is your purpose in life, what values you hold close to your heart, and what gets you perked up.

When you agree to be guided by your Higher Self, you choose to be your authentic self, the role that you are supposed to play and the one that is tailor-made to your success.

Here's how you can forge a stronger bond with your Higher Self:

- Get away from the hubbub, and find yourself a quiet place where you can relax and calm down. Your Higher Self can hardly make itself heard in the midst of all the din of the external world.

- Unplug for a while and take a breather from the raucous world of social media.

- Still your mind to hear the voice of your Higher Self. Practice meditating daily to still your mind in the midst of din.

- Be in the moment. Take your mind off worries and fears about the future and regrets from the past and concentrate your mental energies on the present. When you are focused, the voice of your Higher Self comes through to you clearly. Read on to learn how you can be mindful of the moment.

3. Believe in your abilities.

Every person in this world has been bestowed with some unique ability. Without exception. Some people realize their abilities when they are young while many others do not learn about their special talents till late in life. Just because you are not minting money from your talents, there is no reason to doubt if you have them.

So why do you think your abilities are not being recognized? Don't blame prospective clients, your competitors, the government, or your co-workers. You are in your own way.

The confident person shows it, in his eyes, the words he chooses to get his messages across, and his gait. The person who is not sure hems and haws when he talks and goes around with shoulders slumped. You may not know it, but we are the mirrors of our thoughts. We may not express it in so many words, but our body language says it all.

So when you don't have confidence in your own abilities, how can you expect the world to have faith in your ability to deliver? Would you go to a doctor who says he is not sure if he can cure you?

Don't blame the world if the gigs fail to land in your lap, your boss doesn't give you the raise, or customers don't come flocking to your store. You are driving them away by projecting an aura of doubt. You have triggered the Law of Attraction alright, but you are attracting wrong vibes into your life by letting your mind spiral into negativity.

Bring back your self-esteem by trusting in your Higher Self and believing in the Law of Attraction. Trust that your

Higher Self will show you the way where your talents can blossom. Believe that the Law of Attraction will work for you.

4. Ignore the negative vibes spread by others around you.

You cannot change the world; it will continue to throw curve balls at you. The economy will continue to be unpredictable. Not all business regulations that come into place will look rosy or work in your favor. The competition will grow stiffer with each passing day.

You cannot change the people around you; they will try to hold you back with their snide remarks, discouraging comments, or negative reactions.

The only way you can keep yourself from being overwhelmed by all the negative vibes threatening to engulf you is to ignore them. Do not let this negative energy swamp your positivity.

Recognize negative vibes when you see one and immediately be on your guard. Don't let your sensitive sub-conscious mind pick up on the negative energies.

When people tell you, "You can't do this," they actually mean that they couldn't do what you are about to embark on. But everybody is a different person. Somebody else may not have succeeded in a venture for a myriad of reasons. But none of these reasons will swing into action in your case. Others may have failed, but there is no reason you won't succeed.

It is also likely that jealousy prompts some people to discourage you from carrying out your dreams. After all, it is a competitive world out there, and your competitors might not be very happy to see you succeed.

Also remember that we live in a society that abhors unconventionality. We are supposed to stick to what is the norm and not venture beyond the boundaries of conventions. So it is natural that bold dreams, daring moves, and innovative and alternative ways of working and living raise eyebrows. So when people say, "You shouldn't do this," dismiss their remarks and carry on with your visionary thinking.

5. Shut out the negative emotions in your mind.

Negative energy has a way of overwhelming us, taking over our minds, and gobbling up our energies. Negative emotions take many forms—fear, prejudice, doubts, and worries.

Most of us fear the unknown. We fear failure and not conforming to society's standards. That is why we worry, fuss over details, and try to micro-manage our lives. We try to live up to society's expectations from us, however, improbable they may be. We regret mistakes from a past that we cannot change and obsess over a future that is uncertain.

Our fears, worries, and obsession with sticking to conventions make us compare ourselves to others and doubt our own abilities. A small setback that is common when you pursue your goals or a slight error that can naturally creep in when you are rushing to meet deadlines sends you into a tizzy! You were cruising along merrily till then, but suddenly you start to doubt if you can continue any further!

We are social animals. We like to stick to our brethren and want to be seen as conforming to group ideals and ideologies. In an effort to honor conventions and especially those that do not serve us, we end up harboring a lot of prejudices. We see the world with jaundiced eyes and begin to believe in society's notions of what constitutes a successful life and who is a failure. The result: we become slaves to other people's aspirations.

The sub-conscious mind nurtures these negative emotions, magnifies them, and throws them our way frequently. The result: we become a bundle of negative energy that is capable of attracting only negative events.

The mind thinks, "I can't," and you really fail. The mind believes, "I am no good," and you actually mess up affairs in your life. The mind harps, "I suck," and you end up falling short of the mark. Your sub-conscious mind is powerful. When it focuses on the negative, that's exactly what you attract into your life.

Change starts with YOU. Only you have the power to tame the wild side of your sub-conscious mind. Do not let it absorb negative energy. Turn it into a powerful shield that can keep away negative vibes. Here are the tips:

- Negative emotions and thoughts will arise; it is natural. Just do not dwell on them. There are many distractions—read an inspirational book or a blog post, talk to a friend, watch a funny movie and get a few good laughs, play with Rover or Sparky, or indulge in your hobby.

- Meditate regularly to calm and strengthen your mind.

- Exercise regularly. It is not only good for your waistline but has also been proven to release a slew of "happy hormones" that lift your mood.

- Consciously dwell on positive thoughts.

- Be mindful of the moment.

6. Show your intention by setting bold goals.

You got the low-down on setting and achieving goals in an earlier section. Setting goals not only keeps you focused but also conveys your intentions to the Universe, so it can trigger the Law of Attraction. The Universe may be your ally, but it is a hard taskmaster. You will not get anything lying down; the grand scheme of the Universe is fair. It wants to know that you are serious about your dreams and won't back out half-way. The goals you set prove your intentions.

The Power of Intention works in tandem with the Law of Attraction. When the Universe is convinced of your intentions, it sets into motion the Law of Attraction that eventually brings riches in your life.

Think of it in this way. Go back to those times when you were a kid. Santa Claus brought you gifts, but you had to behave well for the whole year before that. The workings of the Universe are no different.

7. Chase down your goals obsessively.

You also make clear your intentions by the diligence you show as you pursue your goals. It is not enough to write down your goals and hang it on the refrigerator door. You have to stick to them, rather center your life around them. Here are a few tips:

- If you plan to quit your job soon, start saving from now.

- If you want to launch your own business, start exploring ways to set up shop, market, and attract clients.

- Avoid distractions as you chase your goals. You may not realize this, but social media and television are the biggest time wasters in the modern man's life. You log into Facebook to check what's happening in your friends' lives, and before you know it, you have ended up spending an hour commenting, liking, and chatting with someone or the other who is bound to be up at any ungodly hour in this 24x7 world of ours.

- Banish negative thoughts and emotions from your mind. We not only waste time and lose focus dwelling on these, but these feelings also dampen our spirits and weaken our resolve to follow through with our goals.

- Track your progress and take measures accordingly. A progress chart will keep you on your toes and ensure you do not slack.

8. Celebrate little milestones.

We all need a little pat on the back from time to time to keep us motivated and keep going. And if the world is not willing to hand it to us, we need to reward ourselves.

Follow your goals obsessively, but don't get so caught up with the to-do lists that you overlook the little victories. Celebrate little milestones to assure yourself that you are on the right track and you can do it. Tell yourself that every milestone you reach takes you a step closer to your goals. And when things look bleak, as they are sometimes wont to, remember these milestones to recharge your batteries and carry on.

4.

How to Be Your Best Self

I am not a product of my circumstances. I am a product of my decisions. – Stephen Covey

You want to attract abundance and prosperity in your life. You crave wealth, fame, and loving and nurturing relationships.

So shouldn't you take a course in business management or pick up some skills of trade?

What is it about becoming your "best self" that will attract wealth into your life?

Your "best self" is the highest expression of your potential. It is you living up to your true potential while fulfilling your life's purpose.

The Universe has a grand plan to make the world go round. It has plans for you too. You have been bestowed with certain unique talents, and you are here on this Earth to perform to your full potential and fulfill your unique purpose in life.

Unfortunately, most of us spend our lives without realizing our true potential. Sadly, we underperform and never become our highest selves.

What is Your Best Self?

Your best self is an enlightened and inspired soul that has discovered its purpose in life and is not afraid to boldly reach out for the stars. It bubbles with positivity and optimism and brings in a contagious enthusiasm in all that it does.

Your best self is a spiritually-evolved persona that is connected to the Universe and gleans from this primal source of wisdom and knowledge. Your best self is wise and insightful and leads an authentic life in alignment with its motivations, desires, and dreams.

Your best self exhibits character qualities of the highest order. It is compassionate, empathetic, appreciative, and cares for others' interests and well-being. When you are your best self, you not only realize your true potential but also inspire others to become their best versions.

So before you draft a business plan, invest in stocks and bonds, or quit your job to build a money-minting travel blog, aspire to become your best self. When you vibrate at a higher frequency, you automatically attract influential people, money-making opportunities, and other serendipitous events in your life.

Here's how you can become your best self:

1. Connect to Your Higher Self

You were introduced to your Higher Self, your BFF, in an earlier section.

Your Higher Self is a part of you, but it also connected to the Universe. The Universe, a seat of Higher Consciousness, is all-knowing and wise and has designed a grand scheme to keep the whole world running with clockwork precision.

You also feature in its grand scheme of things. The Universe has a plan for you too. It is the blueprint for your life, and trust that this plan has been chalked out to help you reach your full potential.

Your Higher Self knows what is good for you, your passion and purpose in life, and where lies your fulfillment. Your Higher Self can guide you to realize your true potential. Connect with your Higher Self to receive the guidance.

You have to calm your chattering mind and learn to focus. You have to take the journey inward to connect with your Higher Self. Regular meditation will help you reach this calm state of mind.

Meditation

The core principles and practices of meditation have originated in the Far East, in secluded monasteries perched atop hilltops. For a practice that had been shrouded in obscurity for so many centuries, it is natural that myths would abound.

So here are some meditation myth-busters.

No, meditating will not come in the way of your faith. Meditation may have evolved from Eastern spiritual and philosophical traditions, but it is as secular as any other mind-body healing practice.

No, you don't have to retreat to the top of a mountain, don a robe, sit on the floor in lotus position, and count beads to meditate. You can meditate in your work wear or pajamas. You can meditate while sitting in front of the computer, working out, cooking, lying down, or lazing on the beach. You don't have to buy paraphernalia. Nor do you have to search for a teacher, enroll in a class, and learn complex moves and ideas.

There are quite a few different forms of meditation, but all the different methods are geared towards the same goal—to help you calm your mind and focus before you prepare for your inward journey. Of course, some procedures are more difficult than others and have to be taught by a teacher.

But you can start off with basic mindfulness meditation techniques. You can learn them yourself. Do keep reading.

Mindfulness techniques help you calm your mind and improve focus. Don't worry. You won't go wrong because you can't; practicing mindfulness is no rocket science.

2. **Practice Mindfulness**

Mindfulness means to be in the moment and be consciously but non-judgmentally aware. If the jargons have left you confused, here is how you can break down mindfulness into its components.

Firstly, mindfulness is the simple task of focusing on what is happening NOW and HERE, which is in the present moment right in front of you. It means doing away with all thoughts of the past and the future—regrets from the past or worries about the future. Mindfulness also means concentrating on the HERE and not thinking of what may be happening elsewhere.

Secondly, mindfulness is a conscious choice. In mindfulness meditation, you have to choose to be mindful, or be consciously aware of what is happening now in front of you.

Lastly, mindfulness is a non-judgmental state. You are acutely aware of what is happening, but you don't ascribe positive or negative qualities to the events. For instance, when you watch a movie "mindfully," you don't judge it as being "good" or bad". You focus your attention on what is happening on the screen and notice details like the actors' body language, the lighting, the props, and the setting.

How Does Mindfulness Help You Become Your Best Version?

You learned about the characteristics of the mindfulness state. Here's how being mindful makes you a better person:

- **Mindfulness is an effective productivity tool.** *And how?* When you are mindful, you focus all your mental energies on the task at hand. This ensures you do not miss the critical details of the task.

- **Mindfulness makes you bold and ready to embrace change.** When you focus only on the moment, you are not guided by your fears, anxieties, doubts, or other self-limiting emotions, you can boldly unleash your creativity, innovate, and give shape to your quirky ideas. This makes you an intriguing person and a resourceful and ingenious business partner.

- **Mindfulness makes you a more compassionate person.** When you do not judge a person in front of you by his body language, the words he speaks, or the emotions he displays, you come across as a more compassionate person. When you are not judgmental, you become more empathetic. Compassion and empathy are higher-order mental qualities that you will want to cultivate to become your best version.

How Can You Weave Mindfulness Meditation into Your Daily Life?

Now that you know about all its benefits, you will want to embrace mindfulness wholeheartedly and make it a part of your being and living. Good for you!

You can easily incorporate mindfulness activities in your daily life without disrupting your routine. After all, mindfulness is bringing your conscious non-judgmental attention to the task at hand, which can be gardening, drafting a grant proposal, interacting with a client, jogging around the park, or playing with your kids.

It is easy.

Take a deep breath before embarking on the task and resolve that you will not let your attention waver or dwell on any other event other than what is unfolding right in front of you. Now focus.

If you are eating, notice the aroma and the texture of the food. *Can you make out the spices from the aroma? Is the food leathery in appearance or does it look that it will melt in your mouth?* As you bite into it and chew, notice how the food tastes and the sensations it arouses in you. *Did a fuzzy warmth flood over you or were you hit by a tingling coolness?*

If you are walking or jogging, notice your steps as you pound the turf. Notice how the ground feels under your feet. *Is it soft or hard?* Notice the sensation as your feet hits the ground. *Do you feel as if they will sink in or do they land on the ground hard?* Notice what is happening around you.

Other joggers. Kids playing. Mums pushing their babies sleeping soundly in strollers. The fragrant blooms strewn by the curbside. Take in everything with your senses, but don't put a "pleasant" or "painful" tag to them. Just notice.

Mindful Breathing

You can practice being mindful wherever you are and in whatever you do. For a start, try being mindful of your breath for just a few minutes every day.

1. Relax and sit down comfortably.

2. Continue breathing normally and deeply.

3. Focus on inhaling. Feel the air entering through the nostrils. Notice how your belly expands as you continue to breathe in.

4. Now start exhaling slowly and mindfully.

5. Notice how the air passes out of your body through your nose and your belly contracts.

6. Keep breathing mindfully and as you normally do. Do not try to figure out if you are breathing "correctly." Do not try to change the way you are breathing. Just breathe.

The Challenges of Mindfulness Practices

As you embark on the journey inward with meditation, remember that you cannot master mindfulness practices overnight. After years of multi-tasking, juggling multiple roles, and overbooking ourselves, single-minded focus seems alien to us. So expect the frisky mind to revolt and throw tantrums.

The mind will continuously wander and jump from one thought to another. Be gentle and patient with it. Gently coax it to re-focus on the task at hand. Focusing on your breath usually grounds you.

Keep up the practice; you will tame your mind eventually.

3. Learn to Be in and Go With the Flow

Learn to go with the flow and turn yourself into a productivity ninja.

It always good to work according to a plan. Having a detailed strategy in place keeps you focused. But life does not always unfold according to your plans. Even the most well laid out strategies fail.

The economy is fickle and behaves in unpredictable ways. The business environment changes color dramatically. Political incidents affect the demand-and-supply mechanism in ways you cannot fathom. Even changes in tax laws can force you to go on the back foot.

In such situations, being in a flow helps you tide over the challenges, rethink your plans, and keep going on your success trail.

So what is being in a flow like?

It is a state of mindfulness and acute awareness where you "immerse" yourself in the task at hand undistracted and without fearing outcomes. It is a state where you stop being a control freak and instead, concentrate ONLY on the process of creation. Because you are not worrying about outcomes, you are bolder and feel motivated to unleash your creativity.

Musicians and sportsmen often report "getting into a flow." It is a trance-like state where they lose track of time or what is happening around them. They notice only the track or the field in front of them. They feel only their hands and feet move in perfect sync. They hear only the notes flowing from their instruments.

You too enter into a flow when you are engaged in work that you deeply love or indulge in a cherished hobby. Think of those times when you play with your baby or jot down your thoughts in your journal. Remember watching those re-runs of your favorite TV shows so utterly transfixed that you didn't even hear the bell?

Being mindful of what you do helps you enter into state of flow. It feels like bliss when you are in a flow, and you feel refreshed and rejuvenated when you come out of this state.

"Going with the flow" is an attitude that you can bring to other areas of your life to become more productive and spare yourself stress and anxiety.

Going with the flow is letting go of the control freak in you and switching to an acceptance mode. You accept that you cannot control everything that happens to you and around you, so you give yourself permission to change plans or switch tracks according to the demands of reality. You stop obsessing over ideas, notions, and conventions and tell yourself that it is okay to break rules and reinvent sometimes. You give up your reactionary tendencies and instead, choose to "respond" to events and people in your life.

Life is unpredictable. So are people. Going with the flow helps you become more flexible and adaptable. So you can boldly pursue your dreams assured in the knowledge that you have it in you to tackle any challenge. Remember, we as a species, evolved because we could adapt to change.

4. **Express Gratitude**

Our elders often say, "Count your blessings." They have a reason.

Being grateful raises your vibrations and attracts positive vibes in your life. Gratitude makes you humble. Humility is a virtue that draws in many. Your personal relationships improve when you appreciate the qualities and the presence of your loved ones in your life. Your business partners feel motivated to carry on working with you because they feel valued. You forge stronger bonds with people when you cherish them.

Gratitude also helps you overcome challenges and setbacks and become more resilient. When you realize how blessed you are, you are inspired to get up, pick up the pieces, and carry on marching forward assured in the knowledge that the Universe or your Higher Self will look after you. It will be more motivated to work behind the scenes to further your interests.

Look around you. You have many reasons to be grateful for.

You have a roof over your head. You have the love and support of your family. You have loving and caring friends. You have a secure job that lets you put food on the table, pay the bills, and also take the occasional holiday. Or your business is going great guns.

You should also be grateful for the seemingly "little" things we take for granted—the hot water that gushes out every time you turn on the faucet on a wintry morning, the array of goodies lining your refrigerator, and access to quality healthcare services. Countless millions around the world live in poverty and without the basic supplies of clean water, food, and medicines.

Here's how you can express gratitude for all that you have in life:

- Maintain a gratitude journal. Every morning or before retiring for the day, jot down something that you are grateful for having in your life. Read the journal every once in a while, especially when you feel stressed, afraid, or lonely.

- Think of all the persons who make a difference to your life. Write a thank you note to every one of them. Don't wait for their birthdays, anniversaries, or Friendship Day to express your gratitude. Surprise them with a bunch of flowers or a box of chocolates along with your heartfelt note. You will make their day!

- Express gratitude with your deeds. Run errands for an elderly relative who stood by you during difficult times. Lend money to a friend in distress as a way of saying thank you to him for being your pillar or support.

- Finally, express gratitude to your Higher Self for weaving magic in your life. You can jot down your thank you addressing your Higher Self or send across a silent prayer.

5. Connect With and Appreciate Nature

Mother Nature is a healer. She nurtures life and is full of vibrant positive energy. She is soothing. *Think gurgling mountain brooks, placid lakes, and sweeping, rolling, lush greens.* She is resilient, but She also fights back when pushed into a corner. *Think of the devastating floods She unleashes when Her rivers are dammed or the landslides when Her mountains are eroded.*

When you connect with Nature, you can tap into Her limitless reserves of energy. Her lessons in patience, resilience, and persistence can guide you to develop these stellar character qualities while Her soothing, positive vibes will heal you and still your mind.

Here's how you can connect with Mother Nature and absorb Her positive vibes:

- Get up from the front of the TV or the computer, go out, and retreat into the lap of Nature regularly. Take weekend breaks into the nearby mountains or seaside town. Escape into the woods near your home or walk in the park.

- Be mindful of your surroundings. Notice the color of the leaves. Listen to the thunder clouds or the pitter-patter of rain on the roof. Smell the pine cones. Feel the warmth of the sun on your bare skin or the wind ruffle your hair. Just notice.

- Don't wonder if the sun is too hot or worry if you will catch a cold in the rain. Just keep on noticing non-judgmentally.

- Do not look out for positive vibes to spring out of the trees, the lake, or the mountains and flow into you. DON'T TRY! You will absorb Mother Nature's vibes without even knowing it; they are swirling all around you. Your sub-conscious mind will feel and respond to them automatically.

- Spend time with Sparky, Socks, or Rover. Pets emanate soothing vibes. The melting eyes of your puppy or the antics of your frisky cat will never fail to soothe frayed nerves. Animals are stress-busters and provide hours of loving, loyal companionship.

Gratitude always raises your vibes. Express gratitude for Mother Nature's gifts by caring for Her. You can take care of the environment in many ways:

- Reduce your consumption of non-renewable sources of energy. Look up ways on the Internet to save electricity, gasoline, and water.

- Invest in renewable energy systems for your home or office. But if these are not financially feasible, go in for energy-saving gadgets and appliances. You may not have a solar panel on your roof, but you solar-powered water heater will go a long way in saving electricity. Every little action matters!

- Plant trees in your yard.

- Be mindful of the waste you generate. Nifty measures like composting, using a compost toilet, reusing, and recycling reduce the volume of waste you create and lessen the burden on the landfills.

- Volunteer at your local animal shelter. Your presence, a healing touch, or every dollar you donate can save a hapless life. Open your heart to them, and if you can, consider giving them a loving home.

6. **Remove Mental Clutter**

What does the body need to be healthy? A diet of fresh fruits and vegetables, whole grains, and lean protein. You may relish an occasional hamburger or pizza, but you know that too much will set off the alarm bells. We do not thrive on junk food.

The mind too needs its quota of nutrients.

Your productivity owes much to the state of your mind. You need an alert mind receptive to changes, resilient in the face of setbacks, and capable of blue-sky thinking. You need oodles of positive energy to keep your mind performing optimally.

Negative emotions like fear, anxiety, low self-esteem, jealousy, contempt, and hatred clutter the mind and prevent it from doing its job effectively and to your satisfaction. This is junk for the mind.

A cluttered mind clouds your reasoning abilities, implants seeds of fear and self-doubt in you, and hampers your concentration and ability to focus. As you are about to make your way into the world to seek your fortunes, make sure you declutter your mind first.

Toss out all junk, so you can make way for positive energy to come streaming in. Read on to find out how you can declutter your mind and turn it into a reservoir of strength, wisdom, and insights.

7. **Stay Away from Negative Vibes**

The sub-conscious mind is a sensitive precision tool. It can pick up even subtle vibes moving around you, so you are acutely affected by what is going on around you.

Our moods light up when spring is in the air. We may not have been present during the quarrel, but we sense the tension in the air as soon as we enter the room. The presence of a loved one brings on a smile. We are affected by all the vibes present in the environment. While we are instantly boosted by positive energies, negative vibes bring us down and rob us of our mental powers.

Negative vibes can emanate from a myriad of different sources. You will be surprised to know about some of them;

till now, you probably didn't realize they were sucking out your mental energies:

Negative Emotions

You knew it was coming, didn't you?

Harboring and holding on to negative emotions not only clutters the mind but also keeps you from achieving the prosperity you deserve. These emotions not only send out negative vibes that repulse other people but also prevent the Law of Attraction from working.

Negative emotions are productivity dampeners. They weigh you down and keep you from performing to your full potential.

Negative People

Like the thoughts inside of you, elements in your external environment can also drain your energies. Think of all those people who complain about their lot, criticize your innovative ideas, and try to pull you back by scaring you about outcomes. They are the ones who balk at the idea of throwing societal conventions to the wind to explore uncharted territories.

Stress

Duh, that was a no-brainer!

Just as stress is bad for the body, too much of it is bad for the mind as well. Chronic stress is the inevitable result of our over-booked, always-on lifestyle where we get pulled in all directions and in the process, stretch ourselves too thin.

Stress also comes from dwelling on negative thoughts and emotions.

Stress tires the mental muscles and prevents you from going all out and putting in your best. The result is that you fall short of your goals.

Stuck in a Rut

Stagnancy creates a whirlpool of negative energies that quickly suck you into its cavernous depths. Think of a swampy marshland with putrid smell, and you will get the idea!

A job that you hate but cannot quit because you value security. A toxic relationship that you are clinging on to for fear of being rejected or for the "familiarity is comfort" feeling. A seemingly unending routine of household chores, care-giving duties, and job responsibilities that leaves you feeling exhausted and with no time for relaxing and doing your own thing.

You can be stuck in a rut in many different situations. It is up to you to show the spunk and break free.

Unfinished Tasks and Procrastination

Huh?

You are forgiven for being incredulous. Not many people realize this, but all those tasks that you sweep under the rug hoping to tackle them at an uncertain "later" stay at the back of your mind and poke you occasionally. These to-dos put the brakes on your momentum and prevent you from focusing on the task at hand.

Stop procrastinating and get on with your work. Unfinished work tends to hold you back and misleads the Universe into thinking that you are not showing intention and commitment. Closure feels good and liberating; think of the wave of relief that sweeps over you every time you tick off an item on the to-do list.

8. Connect with Positive Energy

With all the stressors and the toxic people around you and the burden of your negative mindset, you need to recharge your mental batteries from time to time. Thankfully, there is no dearth of positive energies around you and inside of you. Here's how to tap into this boundless reserve of positivity:

- Meditate to connect with your Higher Self, an ocean of endless calm and a limitless reservoir of positive energy.

- Surround yourself with people brimming with positive energy. These people are high on confidence, have the dare to embrace change and innovate, are wise enough to understand that things do not always go by the plan, and possess the mental resilience not to bow down to challenges and failures.

- Read inspirational stories to recharge your batteries. Pick up a book of motivational quotes or an autobiography of a person who has made it big by dint of his talent, perseverance, and hard work.

- Stay away from negative vibes.

- Keep believing in the goodness of your Higher Self and the Law of Attraction.

5.

How to be a Leader

The task of the leader is to get his people from where they are to where they have not been.---Henry A. Kissinger

No man lives on an island. We all need one another to survive and flourish. You have set out to carve out the life of your dreams, but you cannot succeed by being the lone wolf. You need collaborators.

People who will inspire you when the chips are down. People who can be the sounding board to your visionary ideas. People with unique talents and special skills who you can collaborate with to realize your dreams. People who will be your allies. People who share your unique insights, perspectives, and values in life and can guide you towards a life of riches. People with expertise and knowledge who can provide the feedback you need to keep on track.

That's a whole team. Yes, but you will have to steer the ship. After all, it is your life. You should be in the driver's seat.

Not everyone amongst us gets to or needs to take on the mantle of leadership in our lives. Some people don't want to take up this responsibility even if they get a call.

Contrary to popular perception, a leader is not a person who just shouts orders. Rather, the leader has to don many hats.

The leader has to be a *visionary* who can gaze into the future, read trends, and come up with killer strategies that will take him to where his dreams lie.

He has to be a *master manager of people* who can inspire his team members to live authentically, dream big, and reach out for their dreams.

He has to be a *mentor* who can guide his team members to become better versions of themselves as they embark on a journey to the riches.

Lastly, the leader has to also be the *foot soldier* of his team who can be called upon to perform any task, to perfection, always.

Leadership is fraught with challenges.

There are detractors who will try to sabotage your dreams and bring down your morale. You have your own inner demons to contend with. There are the challenges of the job. But the biggest challenge is to unite a motley group of people, spur them to believe in a common goal, keep them together, and guide them as you make your way towards your dream.

Acquiring leadership skills helps you succeed both in your personal and professional lives. As a leader you have the power to bring focus and direction in the lives of some talented people and steer them to believe in and achieve their dreams. You can inspire people to break free from their stagnant lives and live a life on their own terms, free, happy, and content.

The 4 Traits of a Leader

The most effective leader may not be the one who is perched on the soapbox. The most inspirational leader does not always shout orders. The leader may not even be the most visible face in a room full of people. In fact, he may tuck himself away some place quiet honing his skills, reflecting on his actions, and planning for the future.

Leadership styles vary greatly. Some are quiet performers who marshal their men and direct them without raising their voices even by a notch. Some command attention by their sheer physical presence and have men scurrying along to line up behind him. But all great leaders get the job done.

You will immediately recognize a leader when you see him in action. There's no mistaking the four characteristic traits of all inspirational leaders who bring about transformation.

1. Confidence

All great leaders of men have this quality in oodles. You can sense it in their eyes, their voices, and in the way they carry themselves. And it is a wonder that the more challenging the task at hand, the stronger is their courage of conviction. The leader may be up against the whole world that believes he cannot pull it off, but he remains undeterred.

Confidence in leaders stems from a staunch belief in their own abilities. They believe in the power of the Higher Self and know in their hearts that they will be able to muster the necessary courage, strength, and energy to tide over a crisis, if it develops.

All leaders have faith in the nobility and authenticity of their causes. And they wholeheartedly believe that they have the support of the Universe in what they are about to embark on.

The confidence also comes from a belief that their carefully-laid out plans cannot go wrong. All great leaders are also master strategists and meticulous planners with blue-sky visioning. They are not the ones to conjure up airy-fairy, nebulous ideas. Their plans are grounded in reality, devoid of loopholes, and contain strategies to counter every crisis that may possibly arise.

Finally, their confidence comes from a belief in their teams. The great leader is not only confident himself but also inspires confidence in his team members. By believing in them and their abilities, leaders inspire their men to be bold, aim for the sky, and reach their goals.

Here's how you can project an aura of supreme confidence that spurs your men into action:

- Believe in your cause. Believe that the Universe has entrusted you to carry out this task and it is a part of the grand order of things.

- Believe that because you are doing what the Universe has intended for you to do, you have also been bestowed with all the powers needed to carry out the master plan.

- Believe that the Universe has your back.

- Believe in your men.

- Visualize your success and feel the tingling excitement in yourself.

2. Enthusiasm and Passion

Leadership is your ability to inspire others to do something.

Ascanio Pignatelli, leadership coach

The leader may be the quietest person in the team, but you can see the fire burning in his eyes. A leader may be a soft-spoken man, but you cannot miss the ring of enthusiasm in his voice. The leader may be a laidback person, but look at the spring in his steps when he goes about doing his work. Passion and enthusiasm are the hallmarks of all great leaders. They inspire men not so much by their speeches but more by the passion their beings resonate with.

Rousing passion. Bubbling enthusiasm.

These are qualities that sets apart leaders from other men who work for money and with an eye on the trophy that awaits them at the finishing line. But the leaders are in it for what the cause signifies.

A leader believes the goals of a project to be an extension of his ideals. The strategies he draws up are a reflection of his core guiding principles. They do not just bring in their knowledge, experience, and people management skills to a cause. Leaders also bring in an infectious enthusiasm to the work that inspires their followers.

Your passion is palpable. It is infectious. But nonetheless and especially in difficult times, show your passion to spread the enthusiasm.

3. Energy

Great leaders not only brim with lots of positive mental energy. They also have in them almost boundless physical energy.

Whatever be their age or physical capabilities, leaders have the uncanny ability to draw in from a hidden reserve of energy when the going gets tough. They work tirelessly, round the clock, throughout the week, and for months on end. You won't hear complaints about life being unfair or how the world at large has failed to appreciate their worth.

Mahubo Fabulous

Great leaders are willing to take up any work that a project demands. No task is great or small in the eyes of the leader. He only weighs the relevance of the job in the light of the greater goals of the project.

Their energy clearly stems from the passion they harbor for the project. Their energy is contagious and inspires their followers to pull up their socks, put their noses to the grindstone, and burn the midnight oil to bring about results.

Although passion for the project will fuel your energy levels, keep in mind the following pointers:

- Eat nutritiously. Steer clear of junk food and aerated drinks that wreck havoc on your system and rob you of your energy.

- Keep yourself well-hydrated.

- Get rest.

- Whether you are putting in 100-hour work weeks or not, ensure that you snatch some downtime to de-stress. This is not a luxury; you need it to keep going.

- Evaluate the results of your efforts regularly. It would be a shame to realize later on that you went flat out for a lost cause.

4. **Authenticity**

Authenticity has a magnetic appeal. In a world where men try hard to bury their individualities to conform to society's ideals and to buy appreciation, a man who is comfortable in his own skin comes across as a breath of fresh air. Honesty and integrity are also the hallmarks of a true leader.

- An authentic leader does not hide behind a mask. He may possess an additional set of qualities that his followers don't, but he is also not afraid to show his emotions and vulnerabilities.

- He inspires his followers with his genuine passion for a project and NOT with tall claims.

- He leads from the front and walks the talk.

- He exudes confidence, but he is also not shy to admit his mistakes and ask for feedback from his followers.

- The true leader hands out appreciation willingly and generously but can also be a hard taskmaster if circumstances demand so.

- He makes clear his expectations from every team member but himself doesn't hesitate to go the extra mile and beyond the call of duty for the greater good of the project.

- He stands up for his team, the ideals that brought him into this work, and the project he has taken up. His passion and integrity shine through.

Leadership Style: How to Lead from the Front on the Ground

You may have all the qualities of a great leader, but you still need to apply them on the battlefront. A leader is as much about his actions as he is about his personality. So express your finest qualities and keep these in mind to lead your men to success and glory:

- Always let your passion and enthusiasm shine through. Believe in the success of the mission wholeheartedly, so you don't need words to convey your thoughts.

- Actions speak louder than words. Show your commitment to the work you do by willingly taking up any task that your team members do.

- Lead by example. Bring in that same level of excellence in your work that you demand from your team members.

- Treat your men as equals. Listen to and respect their opinions. If you have to do otherwise, patiently explain to them why you chose your stance.

- Keep up the motivation level in your team with regular pep talks.

- As a leader you have to also embark on a journey of self-improvement. Share your tips and lessons with your team members, so they too may take the same route and emerge more confident to take up challenges and resilient in the face of setbacks.

- Teach your team members about the power of the sub-conscious mind and how the Law of Attraction works. Make them realize that they are responsible for their thoughts that in turn, lead to consequences.

- Inspire your team to remain positive by not dwelling on negativity yourself. Always talk to them as if success is just round the corner. Believe this yourself, so your team feels motivated and finds something to look forward to.

- Say *thank you* often and hand out praise in public.

- Be fair. Justice should not be compromised ever.

- Stand up to detractors and naysayers or ignore them. But don't let them bring down the morale of your team with their negative thoughts and statements.

- Be compassionate and show empathy. Try to find out about the particular life situation of your team mates to understand where they come from and how can they be influenced.

Being a leader is a tough balancing act. On the one hand, you have to perform yourself while on the other, you have to lead your team to reach the goals. You not only have to be talented and an expert at what you do but also enhance the skills of your team mates and help them achieve personal excellence. These are all in a day's work for you.

6.

How to Set the Law of Attraction in Motion

Keep your thoughts positive, because your thoughts become your words. Keep your words positive, because your words become your behaviours. Keep your behaviours positive, because your behaviours become your habits. Keep your habits positive, because your habits become your values. Keep your values positive, because your values become your destiny.--Ghandi

Once in a while, a book or a movie comes out that grabs us by our throats, makes us sit up and take notice, shakes up our core beliefs, and forces us to rethink the way we had been living and doing things. *The Secret,* both the movie and the book, brought about such an upheaval in the lives of many amongst us.

The Secret unveiled a powerful world of possibilities in front of us. It is a world where reality, as you know it is now, is an illusion. Yes, you read right. The reality that you believe in is an ILLUSION. It is a reality that the world at large wants you to believe in; it is NOT real.

The world may want you to believe that you cannot escape your station in life, but this is not reality. Or else, why do you think one person triumphs over poverty while another person remains trapped in it for life?

The world may want you to believe that the sunset years of a person should be spent lazing in the backyard watching their grandchildren play. But there are countless men and women for whom life begins at 60. They take up new hobbies, go off on wilderness treks, and some even set up their own businesses.

The world may want you to believe that you cannot become rich by writing. But look at all those bloggers who are making six figures from their blogs or the authors who turn out best-sellers with enviable regularity. They prove that the "reality" that writers cannot be rich is actually a myth.

What is real is that YOU can CREATE your own REALITY. In this grand scheme of the Universe, you don't have to be content with less than what you deserve. You can tap into the great power that has been given to you to take back control of your life. You can use this power to burst through the bubble of reality and create your own life, just as you wish to see it.

The power lies in your sub-conscious mind, and it works by triggering the Law of Attraction into motion.

Mahubo Fabulous

The Power of the Sub-Conscious Mind

What you are about to read is not mumbo-jumbo but hard science that has been proved beyond a shadow of doubt.

The sub-conscious mind is infinitely more powerful than the conscious mind. Here's an estimate of the power of the sub-conscious mind.

You learned to walk when you were a toddler. You learned how to put one foot in front of the other, swing your arms, and balance yourself as you took each step. As a kid who was just learning to walk on his own without help, you had to recall each step in your mind and play it out as you gingerly made your way forward.

Walking is now second nature to you. Now when you walk, do you rehearse each step in your mind? Do you have to remind yourself to swing your arms as you put one foot in front of the other? You don't.

Your sub-conscious mind had recorded and stored all the steps of walking. With this memory, it now directs your limbs to carry out the motions without you needing to even pay attention. Your conscious mind is left free to focus on the sights and sounds around you as you walk.

Walking was just one example. Your sub-conscious mind stores a myriad of such information in its bowels. From walking to eating to using the power drill to climbing stairs and swimming, your sub-conscious mind is the storehouse of various bits and pieces of information strung together in a coherent whole to help you carry out the repetitive tasks in your daily life. There is actually no limit to how much information the sub-conscious mind can hold. So there is no limit to the number of tasks you can learn and carry out.

The sub-conscious mind takes over the workings of the conscious mind in many different areas of your life. The habits and attitudes you have learned, the thought patterns you harbor, and the belief systems that guide you are all stored in the sub-conscious mind. What you put into the sub-conscious mind directs your actions in daily life, colors your judgment, and makes you interpret the world around you in unique ways.

When you were a kid, you were told lying is bad. Your parents and teachers taught you not to lie. You got scolded for even the tiniest of fibs you uttered. You read stories of how bad boys got punished for lying. Over the years, this lesson got ingrained in your sub-conscious mind, and now, you cannot say anything but the truth.

Unfortunately, the sub-conscious mind cannot distinguish between positive and negative inputs. So it also picks up on the subtle negative energies that hover around you and all the noxious emotions and thought patterns that you feed it with.

Your parents and teachers constantly told you that you should not go near water—swimming pools, ponds, rivers, and the sea. Some grown-ups in your life also made sure you obeyed them by telling you stories of all the nasty creatures and monsters that infested the waters of the pond in the woods behind your house. They probably had your wellbeing in mind when they issued these diktats, but your sub-conscious mind got the idea that being around waters is dangerous. So you are afraid of water even today.

You do not take beach vacations. The swimming pool in your backyard remains dry throughout the year. Worse, you have transferred your fear to your kids, so they stand and watch when their friends splash around merrily in the lake.

The sub-conscious mind is so powerful that it can channel your life and take it where you want it to go. So it is natural that you will want to feed it with thoughts and habits that work to your advantage.

Here the Law of Attraction comes into play.

The Law of Attraction and the Sub-Conscious Mind

Like attracts like. How often have we heard this phrase? Or how often have you seen it come true in the lives of those around you?

BFFs share hobbies and passions. Or are they BFFs because they have interests in common? *Or is it a coincidence?*

You meet a publisher at your friend's place just after you complete writing your debut novel. *Serendipity, you would say.*

Many people dream of launching their own businesses but are afraid to leave the security of their 9-to-5 jobs. So they stick around, slogging away at their desks but hating their jobs till the day they get the pink slip. Then they are compelled to actually start their own business, the one they had been dreaming about for years. Look around you; there are countless such stories where circumstances compel otherwise risk-averse individuals to take bold steps. *Do you want to know who pulled the strings from the wings?*

Chance. Coincidence. Luck. Call it by any name, it is actually the Universe making things happen in your life. And why is the Universe so obliging? Because it loves you and wants you to fulfill your full potential.

Your wants and desires are deeply embedded inside your sub-conscious mind. But you don't have to shout from the rooftop to make them known to the Universe. After all, the sub-conscious mind or your Higher Self is connected to the Universe. When the Universe learns about your deepest and most cherished dreams and sees your sincere intentions, it moves around the pieces on the game board to help you reach your dreams.

And how can the Universe grant all that you want from your life? It lets loose the Law of Attraction.

How Does the Law of Attraction Work?

The Universe is simmering with energy. All living beings and even inanimate objects exude energy. You too emanate a distinct vibration. You vibrate at a specific frequency that is harmonious with some energies but discordant with others. So naturally, you attract energies that vibrate at the same frequency as you do. *Remember, like attracts like.*

Positive thoughts about reaping riches, earning your financial freedom, and becoming famous attract opportunities for you to make money and earn fame. *And how?*

When your sub-conscious mind focuses on these thoughts, you begin to vibrate at a certain frequency. For instance, you bake great cakes and dream of quitting your boring and grueling desk job someday, if only you can find a way to earn money by whipping up cakes and pies. Your dreams vibrate at a certain frequency. Your energies are like *feelers* that search for harmonious vibes to latch on to.

Then there is a restaurant owner who wants to add baked goodies in the menu to keep his clientele interested. His dreams and goals pulsate with an energy that is similar to yours.

The Universe now steps into the game and kicks off the Law of Attraction.

The Universe senses how keen you two souls are to reach your dreams. So it plots and plans to conjure up opportunities where you cross paths. An acquaintance who loved your apple pie introduces you to the restaurant owner who happens to be her fiancé. Or you two meet at a community soup kitchen, get to know each other, and discover your passions and visions. *And bingo, there is magic!*

When you wish for things for things to happen, you actually begin to script your own reality. The Universe helps you by weaving the pieces of your dreams to create a rosy picture.

How to Make the Law of Attraction Work

The Universe is benevolent, and it wants to help you fulfill your dreams by making the Law of Attraction work. But it wants to first test out your resolve and determination. In other words, the Universe wants to know if you have it in you to keep going till the finish.

You have to show the intention. Here's how to trigger the Law of Attraction in your life:

1. Clear out mental clutter to make way for positive thoughts.

This is the first step as you get ready to usher in any sort of sustainable positive change in your life. After all, you now know how the mind rules the body and can shape your life.

So why do you need to concentrate on clearing mental clutter?

Why can't you just get on with making the Law of Attraction work in your life?

That's because the Law of Attraction can also backfire if you do not focus on positive thoughts. The Law works by attracting into your life all that your mind focuses on. It cannot discriminate between what is good for you and what you want to keep out from your life. So if you dwell on negative thoughts—*I am poor, I am ill,* or, *My job sucks—* you will end up inviting poverty, ill-health, and more job stress in your life. You have to guide the Universe to make it take you where you want to go.

You want riches? Focus your mind on having more money. Think about all the things you can buy with the money, and NOT what you lack.

You want to bag a plum job or get the corner office? Then focus your mind on a fat paycheck. Think about all those tasks you would be expected to perform when you are promoted. You may hate your job now, but do NOT think about pushy bosses, back-stabbing co-workers, and punishing deadlines. Else you will attract more of these people and unhappy situations in your life.

In other words, don't mislead the Universe by focusing on what you don't want in your life.

Think about your attic or any other area in your home where you have let clutter pile up.

Old newspapers stacked up to the ceiling. Outdated receipts and coupons spilling out of drawers and cabinets. Unfinished DIY projects strewn all about the floor. Craft supplies that you don't intend to use anytime soon. Do you think you can fish out anything from this clutter?

It is the same with the mind. If you clutter it with negative thoughts and emotions, the Universe will have a hard time figuring out what your wants are. It is likely that the Universe will end up mistaking your negative thoughts as your wants. *Scary, huh?*

So keep out the clutter from your mind to make way for positive thoughts to flood in and fill you up. Here's the roadmap:

a. Still your mind.

You learned about various meditation techniques in an earlier section. Practice them daily to tap into the powerful reserves of silence and calmness inside you. Make stillness a part of you.

The beauty of these methods is that you don't need to train under a guru, learn hard-to-figure-out philosophical ideas, and take time out from your busy schedule to squeeze in a session. You can concentrate on your breath as you wait for your doctor's appointment or at the signals. Even a 10-minute stroll through the park or in the woods behind your house will calm you.

You can be mindful doing any task, so every task you becomes an exercise in mindfulness meditation. So mindfulness is easy to incorporate in your life.

b. Learn to focus.

Your mindfulness exercises, whether you are gardening or writing a grant proposal, will help you learn to focus on the task at hand without freaking out over outcomes. With practice comes perfection. So keep up your mindfulness exercises; being in the moment will eventually become your second nature.

The mindfulness practices you employ in your daily life will help you create a mindset that lets you detach yourself easily from what is happening around you and inside of you. Learning to detach yourself from the outcomes of your actions and not ruminating on the past are challenging. But learning to detach yourself from negative emotions like fear, anger, and disgust is tougher. A calm and focused mind will help you master your emotions.

c. Detach yourself from your negative emotions.

Detaching yourself from your emotions and prejudices reveals unique and relevant insights that were earlier hidden from view. You realize, "effortlessly," that biases and preferences are actually tools of the human mind to color your perception of the present. There is nothing inherently "good" or "bad" in a person or a situation. It is your mind, shaped by learning, experience, and culture, that ascribes these qualities and then breaks into a sweat over them.

Here's how you can practice detachment in your emotional life:

- Relax and calm your mind.

- Concentrate on the emotion that arises naturally in you at that moment. Don't try to pull up any particular thought. The memory of the brusqueness of the traffic sergeant earlier in the day may come up in your mind and disturb you. *Let it be.* The hurt of a job application that was rejected may come up to haunt you. *Let it be.*

- Do not dwell on the emotion. Do not think about it. Don't judge it. Don't try to delve into whatever it was that triggered the emotion in the first place. Just "watch" the emotion, as you watch a movie or stare at the pond as you sit on the park bench.

- Whatever be the emotion your mind is churning out and howsoever dark it may be, tell yourself that it is only human to harbor negative thoughts. It is natural for the mind to go through emotional highs and lows and experience the whole gamut of thoughts from positive to negative.

- LET GO of the emotion. Of course, "letting go" does not mean you have to fight with your mind and make it brush off the thought. Let that niggling thought melt away as naturally as it had floated into your mind. It will; the human mind is notorious for its fickleness. It jumps from one thought to another. It is we who choose to dwell on these thoughts, color them with our biases and attitudes, and make ourselves more miserable.

Rome was not built in a day. So remember that you can't learn detachment overnight. The mind will not let go of its control easily. Be patient.

2. Set positive affirmations. Repeat them often.

Mindfulness practices help you empty your mind of clutter. Now it is time to invite positive thoughts that tell the Universe what it is that you want from life. Set positive affirmations, and repeat them often.

When a horse cart goes over the same path year after year, the tire tracks get etched into the ground. But if the cart changes route, the older tire marks gradually fade away.

Repeating positive affirmations helps you climb out from the mental rut you had fallen into by thinking negatively over the years. Replace the *"I am no good"* with *"I can do this"* or the *"I suck at everything"* with *"I can make millions if I wish."* Let your sunny side take over the negative and fatalistic mindset that you have developed over the years. Project your most confident and upbeat self to the Universe and demand what you deserve.

Here's how you can set positive emotions:

- Ponder over the version of life you want for yourself. *Do you want to be rich? Do you want financial independence, so you never have to work for a boss again? Do you want to retire with a tidy nest egg stashed away somewhere? A house? The latest car in the market? The money to travel abroad often?*

- Choose your positive affirmations based on your aspirations.

- Repeat them often. Either mumble them, or write out the thoughts in a piece of paper and stare at them.

- Focus on every word of the affirmation as you speak or read it.

- Believe in the words and feel the emotions that arise.

- Keep up the practice for about two weeks to let your sub-conscious mind get into the groove and send out positive thoughts to the Universe.

3. Visualize the reality you want to create. Feel it.

The Secret flew off the store shelves when it came out. People still gobble it up, fascinated by the world of opportunities the book opens up to them. But the book fires the imagination of countless millions around the world also because it provides a concrete roadmap that will empower them to take charge of their lives.

What is more, these are not airy-fairy ways that are hard to fathom, dubious in nature, and inconvenient to carry out. They are *practical* because you don't have to retreat to a mountaintop and meditate. They are *doable* because you don't have to enroll in a class or buy DVDs to learn complicated procedures. They are *rooted in solid logic* because you tap into the proven powers of the sub-conscious mind.

According to *The Secret*, creative visualization alters your reality to make it fit your dreams. You can visualize abundance and attract money, success, fame, and fortune in your life. You can visualize prosperity and attract the good things in life—your dream house, a fleet of gleaming cars, a luxurious yacht, designer clothes and accessories, sparkling diamonds, and everything else that screams wealth, lots of it.

There are two steps to the creative visualization method—visualizing the reality you want for yourself and believing in it, so you can feel the reality.

Visualize

Visualizing your dreams means to see them come true in your mind's eye.

You want to be rich? Visualize yourself signing multi-million dollar contracts with your clients.

You want to quit your job and enjoy your independence without having to worry about paying the bills? Visualize yourself earning pots of money doing what you love—blogging about your passion, traveling, cooking, or playing a sport.

You want to live the high life? Visualize yourself hobnobbing with the Who's-who of the society, driving to posh clubs in your own luxury vehicle, and throwing lavish parties in your palatial mansion.

Visualizing is daydreaming, of sorts. But while in daydreaming, you let your mind wander to where it pleases, in creative visualization, you take the lead and guide your mind to conjure up meaningful visions. So don't be afraid to dream big and plan many exciting adventures. It is your life, and it is time you called the shots.

Believe and Feel

However, visualization alone will not rouse the Universe. It needs more show of conviction from you before it will set the Law of Attraction in motion. So when you VISUALIZE, also BELIEVE that what you see is your reality. And as you believe it, FEEL the emotions that rise within you.

Visualizing that dream house of yours? Believe that you live in that house. In your mind's eye, take a tour of your new home. Marvel at the ornate décor. Smell the fresh flowers. Enter the sprawling kitchen and "see" your family seated at the dinner table, enjoying a lavish spread. Join them and share a few laughs before you move out to the porch. Gaze at the lawn in front you and admire the bright spring blooms. Be happy. Feel contented. Be inspired.

Visualizing riches? "See" yourself quitting your job to launch your own business. "See" your Mom-and-Pop store turn into a mega chain with outlets all over the country. Feel a wave of freedom and satisfaction flood you. "See" yourself working in your home office and getting swamped by plum offers from clients. Smile and be proud of your achievements. Visualize some fat checks or lumps of money. "See" yourself splurging on designer clothes and shoes and taking cruise vacations. Feel excited. Make plans for the next big buy.

Feeling the emotions associated with your dreams triggers the Law of Attraction in a unique way. The sub-conscious mind cannot fathom the difference between what's real and what's in the mind. So when you make it "see" the visuals of your abundance and prosperity, it takes them for real. The accompanying feelings you churn up only bolsters this sense of realness. The sub-conscious mind sends out powerful feelers, the Universe receives them, and thus convinced, it throws some magic your way. Be prepared for amazing coincidences and chance meetings that turn into lifelong and fulfilling partnerships!

4. Be grateful.

The Secret teaches us another way to attract abundance in our lives—through gratitude. You should be grateful for all that you have in your life.

And what do you have? The abundance you visualized just now. You have prosperity and more opportunities for growth, and you "saw" them in your mind's eye. You "felt" the surge of excitement and the warm fuzzies of happiness and contentment when you visualized your abundance.

So now that you have realized your dreams are "real," isn't it natural that you should be grateful to the Universe. The Universe is benevolent, but it too loves a pat on the back occasionally. A heartfelt *thank you* from you motivates it to work more to help you reach your goals.

How should you thank your benefactor is a personal choice, but here are some ways to get your message across to the Universe:

- Use your meditation sessions to focus on gratitude.

- Write an affirmation and read it aloud, focusing on every word and feeling it deeply.

- Make gratitude a part of your mental state. Your sub-conscious mind will ensure the Universe gets the message.

The Law of Attraction is a powerful tool in your arsenal to attract whatever you want in your life. But like all other tools, you have to learn to use it the right way. And like all other tools, you have to use it often to keep the edges sharp.

Every tool comes with its own instruction manual. You just got the low-down on how to use the Law of Attraction. You might want to jot down the points to make your own spiritual how-to list.

7.

How to Grow Money Like a Tree

He who does not economize will have to agonize.—
Confucius

What does financial freedom mean to you?

Not working in a job that you hate while still earning enough to pay the bills, go on an annual vacation, and build a tidy nest egg that will let you live comfortably in your sunset years.

Actually having a tidy nest egg stashed away somewhere.

Not living from paycheck to paycheck.

Earning doing what you love without a boss or tight deadlines breathing down your neck.

Working at a job that you love and one that provides ample opportunities to grow—take home a six-figure salary and bag the corner office.

Becoming debt-free.

Retiring early to a life of security, comfort, and peace.

Carving out the peace of mind that comes from knowing that you have enough money stashed away in your bank that will see you through three months even if you don't work.

Knowing that you are earning and saving enough to send your kids to college debt-free and put away money for rainy days.

We all harbor different ideas about financial freedom. It is natural because we are all different from one another. Our needs are different. We have different priorities in life. Our life situations vary greatly. And most importantly, we have different dreams.

But whether you are in a white-collar job or run your own business, you definitely want to carve out a life of riches where you don't have to worry about money any more. Whatever we do right now to earn our living and whatever we want to do for the rest of our lives to keep the money flowing in, we all want to be spared the niggling worries about how we are going to pay the bills, how to squeeze the tiniest bit of comfort or luxury into a tight budget, and how to create a monetary security net without slogging away at our boring desk jobs, working multiple punishing shifts, or living like a pauper for the rest of our lives.

For most of us, financial freedom is not just about having a hefty bank balance. It is also about having the peace of mind knowing that we don't have to worry about money for the rest of our lives.

We live in difficult times.

Mahubo Fabulous

The economy is volatile. What looks hunky-dory right now can change in an instant, and we could be deep in the throes of another recession in the very next moment. Most of us still remember the scares of the recession. We know many who still bear the scars of the meltdown. We all know of someone who lost his job during those trying times or had to foreclose his dream house.

We have overcome those bleak times, but the economy is fickle. The market forces do not always go by what the copybooks prescribe.

The ways of our present-day inter-connected world are weird. We could be cruising along merrily one moment and then find ourselves fighting to save our jobs and homes the very next moment. And why? Maybe because a European country has plunged into recession or probably war has broken out in some other part of the world.

And then there are the financial battles back home that never seem to end. Rising healthcare costs, soaring prices of gas, utilities becoming more expensive, and inflation eating away at our savings. We never seem to be able to relax around money. And we never seem to have enough of it.

In such unpredictable times, you can never be too prepared. Besides, we all know about the stresses of having to make do with too little money. Having to go without the things we love. Stalling holiday plans. Paring down lifestyles. Downsizing. And the pain, frustration, and depression of seeing our homes taken away from us. Financial stresses, poverty, and deprivation take a toll on our relationships and our mental health.

There is only one solution: get rich.

Create a sound and sustainable financial plan that you can stick to. Create steady streams of income that will see you through difficult times. Build habits and sustain them to manage your money better.

Read on to find out how you can grow money like a tree.

1. Spend Less

For many people, their financial woes stem not from having too little money but from spending more than their means. The golden rule of money-making is: spend less than you earn.

Here are some tips to help you make your dollar stretch without depriving yourself:

Track personal and household expenses.

Double-income households. Multiple credit cards. Shopping online. Repaying debts. Your hard-earned money flows out through multiple channels. Keeping up can be challenging. But you have to know where your money is going to decide if you need to curb spending or take up another job to make ends meet.

Track your expenses. Enlist your partner's support in this, so you know about the household expenses. Here's how:

- List all the fixed costs for the month. These include rental and/or mortgage payments, debt repayments, payment for childcare services, and any child or spousal support money you may pay. Unfortunately, you cannot do much to bring down these expenses.

- List the essential expenses. These include grocery bills, the money you pay for the utilities, gasoline, credit card bills, and medical expenses.

- List recreational expenses. Don't feel guilty about taking time out to indulge in fun. We all need to recharge our batteries every once in a while. You only have to figure out if you are spending more than you can afford on this front. After all, there are countless ways to have fun without breaking the bank.

- List the expenses you incur to maintain your investment portfolio. This is also the right time to mull over the returns from these investments and figure out the feasibility of each.

- List all the other expenses that you incur in a month. You may not spend on these every month, but keeping track helps. Who knows, you might just realize that you tend to spend inordinate amounts on gifts or that that the occasional spa session is actually messing up your finances.

Curb impulsive spending.

The bane of our existence!

But it is the times we live in. We live in a consumerist society that teaches us to equate stuff with happiness. The marketers want us to find value in goods. Look at all the commercials dancing on the TV or staring at you from the billboards. *And what are the messages they have for you?*

The only way to have fun with your family is to go out for a drive in a big, shiny, and expensive car.

New clothes and bags give you happiness. Peace is in pizzas, colas, chocolates, and burgers.

The beautiful woman is one who has an impossibly-thin figure, sports a mane of shiny, bouncy hair, and has flawless skin.

You should woo your beloved with nothing less than diamonds or a vacation in an exclusive seaside resort.

Success is an expensively-done up condo, several cars in the garage, and designer clothes.

Good times are party times where the champagne flows freely.

And after they have bombarded you with these messages, they fill up the store shelves with goodies, lots of them. So when you go out shopping, you are tempted to splurge on a designer bag or gobble up junk food because your sub-conscious mind remembers all those messages. Such is the compelling power of those messages that you even feel happy with your buys. That's retail therapy for you, and it is as real a problem as pain in the knees or a physical disease.

You cannot stop the marketers from airing the commercials. Goods will continue to spill over from the store shelves. Instead, you have to curb your impulsive spending habits. The root cause is in your mind.

- Train the mind to recognize the difference between a need and a want.

- We often splurge on stuff when we are stressed out or feel too tired to flex our mental muscles, so meditate to still and strengthen your mind.

- If you have to go shopping, steer clear of the glittering malls and large departmental stores where all the temptations are laid out. Instead go to the flea market or raid the neighborhood departmental store.

- Shop with a list in hand. This will help you stay focused.

- Do not roam around endlessly through the aisles. You will end up picking a lot of stuff that you "think" you can't do without.

- Keep a gratitude journal. Impulsive spending often stems from a place of want. Discontentment or a feeling that something is missing from our lives causes us to feel depressed. We then try to "fill up" our lives with stuff. Your gratitude journal will remind you what you have in life and how blessed you are, so you don't feel the need to go in for a retail therapy.

- Find peace in giving. Donate money, unused stuff, or your time to those in need. Recognizing the needs of other people will also keep you from dwelling on your own wants.

Go shopping but without the plastic.

If you can, ditch the plastic and pay with money.

The credit card may have brought in oodles of convenience in our lives, but it has also escalated our mindless spending habits. When we buy on credit, we usually cannot keep track of our expenses. We get the shock of our lives when the bill arrives at the end of the month. So don't carry the credit card *(or any other plastic for that matter)* when you go out to shop.

When you have to actually shell out money to pay for the stuff you buy, you can track your expenses *(We need a reality check sometimes.)* and also keep a tight rein on your spending.

Build healthy habits.

Eh? What's that got to do with spending less?

Think of all the doctor visits you make throughout the year or the pills you pop in. *You got the idea, right?*

Eating junk food regularly not only adds to your waistline but also erodes your body's immunity system. The gym membership is costly. The niggling back pain or your tendency to catch every bug that is going around costs hundreds of dollars every year in over-the-counter medications.

Unhealthy lifestyle habits like not exercising, smoking, and drinking can trigger a host of grave diseases like hypertension, diabetes, cardiac ailments, and kidney and liver diseases. And, healthcare is expensive these days.

You can cut down on your healthcare bills and medicinal expenses by forming healthy habits. What is more, these healthy habits will keep you fit and energetic for years to come. When you brim with energy, you can explore more ways of making money, but more on this later.

Create a monthly budget and stick to it.

Now that you have tracked your expenses, you can create a monthly budget and allocate funds for each activity and need. Your fixed costs remain unaltered.

Allocate funds for groceries, recreational activities, gasoline expenses, and any other cause you want to pursue. Then resolve to stick to this budget, come what may. This will require immense discipline, but practice makes a man perfect!

If you discover that you have used up the funds you had allocated for recreational activities by the middle of the month, don't siphon off money from other funds. Instead, do without a trip to the cinemas and watch a re-run on the TV instead. If your gasoline expenses overshoot the budget, take the bus or the subway to work.

But sticking to a budget does not mean you have to deprive yourself. If you create a realistic but restrained budget, you won't have to skimp to save.

2. Save More

The wise men say that every dollar saved is a dollar earned. Spending less and saving more helps you build funds for your personal projects without needing to take up a second job or work multiple shifts. If you foresee a need for considerable liquid cash in the coming months, say to stock up on holiday inventories for your store or to undergo an uninsured medical procedure, you can start saving from now on. Who knows, you might even manage to save up enough, so you don't have to take a loan.

Saving is an excellent money management habit. It has multiple short- and long-term benefits. Build this habit.

Here are some tips on how to save more money without feeling deprived.

Shop smart.

You cannot stay away from the stores and malls for fear of splurging. You have to tame your mind, so it does not talk you into splurging. Here are some tips to help you keep away from splurging when you are actually inside the store and staring at the goodies galore:

- Build the habit of leaving your credit card at home before you head out to the stores.

- Draw up a shopping list and carry only so much money on you as you will need to buy the items on the list. This ensures that even if temptation gets the better of you, you won't have much money to splurge on unnecessary items.

- Don't wander aimlessly through the aisles peeking at the goods lined up on the shelf. Stay focused and pick up the items on your shopping list first before you explore the store.

- Look out for discounts. Hunt down bargain sales. Choose the flea market over a designer boutique.

- Buy essential items in bulk. Buying in bulk always turns out to be cheaper than buying one or two pieces at a time. Besides, you also get to save on the trips to the store when you buy in bulk.

Eat out less.

You may not realize this, but eating out is more expensive than rustling up a meal at home. While it is true that you are spared all the hassles and efforts of shopping for the ingredients, chopping vegetables, and doing the cooking when you go out to dine or order food home, your wallet takes a hit. At the end of a hard day's work, it does feel temping to take the easy way out, but cooking ceases to be a back-breaking chore if you follow the following tips:

- Keep your refrigerator always packed with the ingredients to cook a quick meal, a power-packed smoothie, or a sandwich. This ensures you don't have an excuse to eat out or order food.

- Prepare food beforehand, ideally just after you are back from grocery shopping. This saves you time and effort when you have to cook.

- Prepare lots of food at once and store in batches.

- Brownbag your lunch.

- Use the slow cooker or the crockpot. You don't have to chop the vegetables finely if you use the slow cooker, and you are spared the strain of standing, watching over, and stirring the food as is the case when you cook on the stovetop.

- Try freezing fruits and vegetables at home because buying them turns out to be a more expensive option. Besides, store-bought frozen food is loaded with chemicals and preservatives that are harmful for you.

Look up the Internet to find the guidelines on freezing.

Declutter your home.

No, you don't have to pare down to five dresses and ten books! But minimalism has its advantages. Clutter is an eyesore and is stressful. Try locating and extracting things you need from a pile of old papers and unread books stacked high up to the ceiling, shelves spilling over with stuff, and drawers full of old receipts and torn magazines.

Clutter is wasteful too. You have to spend considerable money, time, and effort to maintain your cluttered house. Besides, clutter takes up valuable space, so you have to rent storage space to stash away your stuff that, unfortunately, can comprise more clutter.

Householders on a decluttering mission often complain that they cannot figure out what is clutter. At first glance, almost every object seems useful—that's the *I-would-need-it-someday* mentality.

So here's a nifty tip to help you nail down what is clutter. If you are unsure if something is clutter or not, pack it and stash it away some place where you cannot see it. If you don't use it for about two weeks or a month, be assured that you will never have any use for it. Your life did not come to a standstill, so you can toss it away, donate it, or sell it.

Decluttering not only feels liberating, but you can also earn money from the junk that other people might find useful. Put up your stuff on the Internet, on sites like eBay and Craigslist, or arrange for a garage sale. You will be pleasantly surprised to discover how many people are on the lookout for bargains and don't mind buying used stuff.

Reduce. Reuse. Recycle.

This had been the environmentalist's mantra for so long. But you can also save on your utility bills by reducing the amount of waste you generate and reusing and recycling stuff.

The Internet is full of nifty tips to help you find ingenious uses for household "waste." For instance, kitchen scraps can go into the compost bin. You can use old newspapers to make cat litter—the paper won't end up clogging the landfills and you won't have to spend a fortune on commercial litter. Don't throw away cartons and boxes; they make for great storage devices.

Adopt energy-saving practices at home and while driving.

Heating and cooling costs and utility bills comprise a lion's share of the domestic expenses in an average American home. Energy-saving practices will not only save the environment but also lessen the drain from your wallet.

And no, saving energy at home doesn't mean you have to install expensive solar- or wind-powered systems. You can save electricity and gasoline with easy-to-follow measures like the following:

- Switch to ENERGY STAR-rated appliances that are designed for maximum energy efficiency.

- Insulate your home to save on heating and cooling costs.

- Make the switch to LED bulbs.

- Turn up the thermostat once in a while and put on an extra layer of warm clothes to save electricity in winter.

- Install water-efficient bathroom and kitchen fixtures.

- Open the windows and let sunlight stream in to keep the room warm during winter. Draw the curtains in summer to prevent the sun from heating up the rooms.

- Switch your gas-guzzling car for a new and more energy-efficient make.

- Ensure that your car always runs on fully-inflated tires. Make sure that air filter is clean and working the way it should.

- Don't speed; slowing down saves gasoline. Also avoid jerky stops and starts.

- Don't idle if you think the stop is going to be more than 30 seconds long. And warming up the car before driving is not necessary.

- Keep your appliances and car in top-notch working order to keep them functioning optimally.

The above are just a few tips on how to save energy and gasoline. There are almost countless other easy ways in which you can save money on your electricity, fuel, and utility bills without incurring any upfront investment. Do look up on the Internet.

3. Build a Money-Making Machine

There was once a time when a 9-to-5 job translated into security for a lifetime. You were assured of your monthly paycheck. You knew how much you would make after a lifetime of working and could dream about retiring in comfort. But not anymore.

We have fallen upon hard times when it comes to the job sector. You can blame it on the whims and fancies of the economy or the inter-connectedness of economies across the world where a regime toppling in one part of the world wrecks havoc on business in another corner. But the chilling reality is that the first casualty of a downturn in the economy is the job sector. You can no longer sit back and rest easy in the thought that you will always have your job to fall back on in times of distress.

Thankfully, there are quite a few ways to supplement your salary, and if you stick with them, some are guaranteed to bring in more money that what you earn from your day job. But wait, this is still not the best thing about these earning opportunities.

The income-earning opportunities that you are about to be let into will make you money even when you are SLEEPING. Or when you are holidaying by the beach or playing with your kids. Set up one of these passive income systems, and you are assured of money flowing in without you having to slog and burn the midnight oil.

Government Bonds and Dividend-Bearing Stocks

Shrug off your fear of the stock market. It is as safe as your day job, and if you can find your way through the maze of stocks, bonds, equities, and debentures, you can earn pots of money here as well.

Contrary to popular opinion, investing in the stock market is not always fraught with high risks. There are quite a low-risk investment options that promise high rates of returns.

Investing in dividend-bearing stocks of stable and reliable companies that have a history of paying out dividends regularly can bring in a steady supply of money. For all its safety, it is still a wise ploy not to put all your eggs in one basket. So invest in the dividend-bearing stocks of more than one company. This also ensures that you can reap benefits should all these companies see spurts in growth and increases in their stock values.

If you would rather be safe in the stock market and are willing to settle for a little less return on your investment, you can go in for treasury inflation-protected securities issued by the government.

The stock market can be difficult to navigate for the novice. So take the advice of a professional to find your footing. You can also take a course to learn the basics of trading in the stock market.

High-Yield Checking or Savings Accounts

Those who like to be safe with their investments have a penchant for stashing away their hard-earned money in savings accounts. Besides, the money saved with a bank is easily accessible. But the interest environment is not always as rosy as you would like it to be.

So you might consider putting away your money in a savings account that has a higher rate of return than that offered by the conventional brick-and-mortar establishments. Consider online banks and credit unions.

Rental Income

You can earn money by renting out assets you already own. For instance, try dabbling in the lucrative real estate market. Consider renting out your house or apartment to earn a tidy sum every month. The rent you can command, of course, depends on the specifications of your property, its location, and the demand for real estate in the neighborhood. Online rent estimator tools will help you calculate how much you can charge for your property.

Zeroing on the perfect tenant can be challenging. Exercise caution, carry out background checks for criminal records, and ask to see credit score reports and references from previous landlords before you give your word and draw up an agreement.

Monetized Blogs and Websites

In an age where the Internet is the favored mode of communication across ages and geographies, it is only natural that there would be ways to earn on this platform by reaching out to millions of people in the world.

If you have information to share that people will find useful, then post the content on a blog or a website and monetize it. You can build a blog or website on a subject that you are passionate about or have expert knowledge of. This ensures that you don't have to spend too much time *(or none at all)* hunting for information or rustling up titles.

Here's how you can build a blog or a website that brings you a six-figure income:

- **Implement Google AdSense.** Google AdSense is an established way to earn money from your blog or website. You can display text, image-, and/or text-and-image based ads and earn from the clicks on them. The Google AdSense program virtually *(no pun intended)* rains in money once your blog is up and running and you have established yourself as somewhat of an authority in your niche with a loyal following.

- **Go in for affiliate marketing programs.** Use your blog/website and your clout to promote useful products and services as an affiliate partner. Partner with industry thought leaders, innovators, and inspirational personalities who have value to provide to your readers and in the process, earn from the association.

- **Become a member of the Amazon Affiliate program.** If you are a member of this program and can direct visitors from your blog to Amazon's shopping platform and convince them to buy a product, you can earn up to 15 percent of the sale price.

- **Attract ads.** If your website or blog draws large crowds, you can persuade local and national businesses to advertise on your site. They will only be too happy to tap into a new audience base without having to shell out a fortune on marketing efforts. Use the Google Analytics tool to find the footfall on your site.

Informational Products

If you are an authority on a subject and have established a credible blog with a sizeable footfall, then try to sell informational products through your site.

You can sell eBooks, podcasts, or videos. Work hard to create a stellar product, and your one-time investment will continue to bring in money through the years. What is more, you don't have to reinvent the wheel always. For instance, you can package the most popular blog posts on your site into a short eBook or take content from existing pages or posts and turn them into podcasts.

4. Invest in a Mentor or Take a Course

Self-improvement is a fulfilling DIY project. But we all need an expert pair of eyes to go over our plans, evaluate our successes, and suggest improvements or novel ways of working.

You work hard to balance your professional and personal lives. And now you are working doubly hard to form great habits, think up new ways to earn money, bring in lifestyle changes to save more money, and preparing to launch your own business. You can't be expected to keep abreast of what's happening in the field of finance, how the stocks are behaving in the market, and how you can tap into evolving technology to make more money.

An expert can help you chalk out feasible financial plans that will align with your goals and help you march forward to realize your dreams. Or you can take a course that dishes the dope on sensible budget planning and financial management. Ensure that you choose a course that contains a lot of tutorials.

As you reach out for your dreams and explore new ways to make money, you will face choices. It will not always be easy to decide. Your mind might trick you into going one way by throwing up fear, anxieties, and self-doubt. Societal expectations or peer pressure can weigh down and color your judgment, and you may end up sacrificing your passions to please others or for the sake of conformity.

When faced with difficult choices, you need an unbiased mind and a neutral outlook to help you decide what is best for your interests.

A life coach can help you chart your true life path in alignment with your passions, values, strengths, and weaknesses. He or she takes the time to understand you—what makes you tick, what are your motivations, what holds you back, and how your life experiences and educational attainments have shaped you. He or she delves into your mind to find out about your passions, life goals, and dreams and learns about your personal and professional obligations.

Human beings are complex individuals. We want many things, all at once. We want to follow our dreams. But we also want to keep working at jobs that we hate, so that the money keeps coming in. We are determined to work hard to make our businesses reap profits, but we also want to take time off to focus on our hobbies that don't bring in money.

A life coach helps you draft a blueprint for your life by tying in all these ends, so you can live the way you want to—without compromises, true to your authentic self, and in alignment with your values.

The rapid expansion of the powers of the Internet and the rise of an inter-connected world have opened up numerous avenues to make money. Yes, you can now grow money like a tree.

You have what it takes to grab the riches. But it is not just about investing smartly, saving more, and spending less. You have to embark on a journey of self-improvement, ditching bad habits, building and sustaining good ones, and learning to express gratitude.

As you work on growing money, you also work on yourself. Be assured, the transformation will be life-changing. You will not only laugh all the way to the bank but also develop habits, attitudes, and thought patterns that will enrich your life in many other ways.

The Last Word

Whoa! We have reached the end of the book.

But did you realize that we talked mostly about you in the book? The money-making tips came right at the end, after you were done with your meditation sessions *(Ideally, you should continue meditating.)*, decluttered your desk, built a healthy eating and exercising routine, invested some money here and there, and ditched your credit card.

So you see, it was actually about YOU.

The secret to grow rich and stay rich is YOU. Of course, Google AdSense helps and becoming an Amazon Affiliate partner increases your income-generation potential. But in the end, it is still about you.

Self-made rich people employ a variety of ways to make their money and build their empires. Some work, some flop. There is no one formula to get rich.

But these people have several character traits in common.

They have mastered the art of controlling their mind's endless mindless chatter. Their tamed minds do not churn up negative thoughts and attitudes.

Such is their control over their minds that they turn into shields in the face of negative emotions and statements hurled at them from people around them.

Their positive energy is palpable and their slew of good habits is inspiring.

They are inspirational leaders of men, who can summon forces, rouse them to action, and make them march confidently towards their goals. These men and women are master planners and insightful strategists who can foresee the future and plan their present accordingly.

Do you notice a pattern? These people worked on their habits, attitudes, and belief patterns before they made their smart investment moves and launched businesses.

Do you want to follow suit? The roadmap is clear.

Master your mind. Radiate positive energy. Dream big and believe they have already come true. Then let the Universe take over.

Opportunities. Connections. Collaborations. Ideas. Deals. Meetings. A world of possibilities will open up in front of you.

For the first time in life, you will get to choose. For the first time in life, you won't have to worry about money. For the first time in life, you can put your interests, passions, and dreams on the front burner and not feel guilty about it.

When you grow rich, your life changes in many ways. Of course, the changes are for the better because this is the beginning of the REAL YOU unfolding itself and waking up to its immense potential.

Congratulations! Your new life has begun. A life of riches and limitless abundance that was yours for the taking for all this time.

About The Author

Mahubo Fabulous is a professional life coach who helps people find and attain their life's purpose and realize their true potential. She combines her deep knowledge and intuitive understanding of human nature to guide her readers to fulfill their dreams and in the process, carve out richer and more meaningful lives for themselves. Mahubo Fabulous lives in Los Angeles, CA with her cat Meeko. You can follow Mahubo Fabulous on the following social media platforms:

FB, Youtube, IG and Twitter: Mahubo Fabulous

Visit: Www.MahuboFabulous.com